To Di

15 MINUTE
pause

A RADICAL REBOOT FOR BUSY PEOPLE

Happy Pausing

Enjoy *M Burke*

MICHELLE BURKE
FROM THE AUTHOR OF
THE VALUABLE OFFICE PROFESSIONAL,
and
LILAMANI DE SILVA

TABLE OF CONTENTS

ACKNOWLEDGMENTS

MICHELLE BURKE

A special thanks to my Dad who taught me the value of living with faith and life to the fullest, to be grateful and laugh along the way. He inspired me by his actions especially after being diagnosed with cancer at age 54, defying the odds by living 20 years past what doctors thought possible. To my Mom who taught me perseverance and having a positive intention is key, to my brother who is an awesome Dad to his kids, Riley, Amelia and Zoe, and his "half-cup full" attitude and support make a difference, to my sister, a loving Mother to her son, Hudson, and for her thoughtfulness and resilience, to my bonus sister, Kelly for her positive outlook and her ability to always make me laugh. To my nieces and nephews who light up my life, to my friends who are like family and keep me grounded and lastly, my colleagues and clients who give me the opportunity to do the work I love. With deep gratitude.

LILAMANI DE SILVA

Special thanks goes to my adorable parents who have shown me how to laugh out loud and taught me what it is to be resilient and optimistic. I am eternally grateful to you for your kindness, love and support. Thanks to my siblings, nieces, nephew and cousins who hold a special place in my heart. You keep me grounded and bring me so much joy. Last and not least my friends, my special extended family.

We want to thank all those who have helped us with bringing *15 Minute Pause* out into the world. Kind thanks goes to our publisher, Jeannie Bruenning for her patience and guidance, Kimberly Hathaway, our publicist, for her expertise and her out of the box thinking, Bridgette Mathews who designed our beautiful cover and graphics, Jennifer Mones who brought life to the Meddler and Player illustrations, Shavon Kiscellus for her imaginative social media content, Josh Schuyler for his creative web design and always coming through in a pinch.

Our sincere gratitude to our friends who lent their ears and advice while we were writing *15 Minute Pause*. Last but not least, to all the busy people who've taken a well-deserved pause.

PREFACE

Over the years, we have traveled back and forth,
we've shared tears of pain and tears of joy, spent
hours chatting over Skype and sent countless emails.
As work/life coaches, we wrote this guidebook to
share our discoveries, tools and insights with you.

Despite the very different lives we have led, we
know that *joy doesn't choose you, you choose it.* It is
not dependent on whether you are rich or poor,
fat or thin, married or single. We've learned
to be deeply grateful, to bless the past and to
be aware of and live fully in the present.

Above all we discovered how important
it is to live a joy-filled life no matter what
challenges show up along the way.

Enjoy!

JOY-FILLED
adj.

Has self-worth. Values self-care and shows
kindness to themselves. Has gratitude, is aware
of joyous moments that show up. Is not stuck
in worry, fear or doubt. Manages stress, engages
life fully and appreciates the present moment.

WHY I MATTER

We all want a more joy-filled and less stressful life. Whether you are juggling work priorities, financial worries, or concerned about child daycare, are you having joyous moments along the way? Imagine how you'd feel if you could take quality time to pause and step off the busy treadmill of life daily. Have you ever had a week or month go by and realized you still haven't taken time off to enjoy life's little pleasures? The truth is that too often, we find ourselves overly stressed, exhausted, and overwhelmed, making it increasingly difficult to take a time out to experience joy in the midst of chaos.

The problem is we've become addicted to our busyness and to our technical devices leaving us operating 24/7 on autopilot. We are so busy being busy, that there is no perceived down time anymore. When did busyness become a competitive sport and life a rush to the finish line? We are literally missing what's happening in our present lives. What makes it more challenging is that our culture promotes and even praises us for being busy. It's no wonder that our stress levels have increased. In fact, according to payscale.com three out of four are in a highly stressed state with over 1 million workers calling in sick every day, costing US employers about $200 billion per year in lost productivity [1].

It begs the question, *what can we do about it?*

The answer is - a *15 Minute Pause*. This pause is defined as a sacred time-out for ourselves. 15 minutes helps us to be present, in the moment. When we are present we are more self-aware and can make better choices. A pause during the busyness helps us to reflect, prioritize, be mindful and notice the joy in our lives.

We are often asked why we wrote this book. We would say we were compelled. We aren't psychologists or therapists, we are two ordinary people, like yourselves. We discovered we didn't have all the answers, rather, we had insights, engaging solutions, and strategies that have been tried and tested, including with Michelle's clients, and received great results.

Michelle is a coach and consultant with over twenty years' experience. She noticed a trend in the workplace, people were working longer hours and taking less time for themselves, including, not taking time-out for lunch. She also noticed how workplaces are becoming increasingly stressful with high pressure deadlines and increased workloads. She shared her insights with her friend, Lilamani.

The conversation began with how busy everyone's lives were and how the increased pace was leaving clients, friends, and ourselves more stressed out and exhausted. Like many people, we've spent hours with friends mulling over stories and exchanging experiences about struggles, love lives, health scares, losses, financial worries, career changes and achievements.

Despite our stressors, we found ways to laugh and appreciate the little things in life. We were surprised how we coped with the various demands and hardships that life inevitably thrusts upon us. We discovered in our conversations that we needed to take regular time-out to recharge, reflect and relax so that we can be kinder to ourselves and therefore take better self-care.

We wondered if taking a time-out was the solution to helping us relieve our stresses. So, we investigated further, and on our journey, we realized that taking time-out to re-energize needed to be easy and doable, because like many of you, our schedules were packed full. We decided to explore this concept with taking 15 minutes of "me time". We reminded each other to regularly take time when we were struggling. And for those who doubt the value of 15 minutes, it adds up to a surprising 91.25 hours a year, a significant quantity of time. Isn't it true that most of us feel we can't take an hour, yet even the busiest amongst us has 15 minutes to spare?

We noticed when we committed to a daily practice of 15 minutes, it allowed us to be reflective, grateful and make better choices. We could see the funny, calming, and meaningful moments in everyday situations — what we call "joyous moments", no matter what ups or downs we are going through.

A daily pause opened our eyes to being present and made us aware of how important it is to give back to ourselves. As we took more time for ourselves, the more joy we noticed along the way. We started paying more attention to the joy we already had in our lives. This helped us to truly appreciate and notice these joyous moments in their various guises. And when we did, we noticed that joy appeared more often; it wasn't found in isolation rather it was an integral part of our lives like an unexpected phone call from a niece, a compliment from a stranger, appreciating the warmth of sunshine on our faces or a spontaneous hug. What's important is to recognize that when our fears, busyness, negative mind chatter, and stress get in the way, it stops us from noticing the good stuff. We believe taking a regular "me" time-out for ourselves has helped us and can do the same for you.

Consider this guide your playbook and coach for life. It is an accumulation of the aha's we've discovered that have helped us put ourselves on our priority list. On our journey, we found out how to be more self-aware, make conscious decisions and pause for fifteen minutes or more every day. We bring these vital ingredients together to create the **i-Matter Equation = Self-Awareness + Conscious Choice +15 Minute Pause.** This is our secret recipe for taking care of ourselves - 15 minutes dedicated to "me" time. The **i-Matter Equation** is personal and, therefore, not a one-size-fits-all-cure. Rather, it is unique to each person. The **i-Matter Equation** reminds you to put yourself at the top of your to-do list because you matter. This book is not about 'fixing yourself', rather it's about taking better care of yourself. Who can do everything and be everything to everybody without refilling their tank?

Self-care is not all bubble baths and decadent desserts. Some decisions might be tough like preparing healthy meals instead of buying take out, breaking a sweat instead of eating a pizza or saying "no" more often, so you can say "yes" to yourself. Long-lasting rewards come to those who take steps to being more self-aware or mindful and can make better choices without self-sabotage. A daily pause will allow you to create the space to reflect and take time out to notice joy.

As we embarked on our journey we asked our friends to join us. Every endeavor needs support. We encourage sharing this experience with your best friend, spouse, mentor or someone who needs to experience more joy, rather than doing it alone (although you certainly will get value if you do). We found that when we shared our experience with someone, we had greater success in making the changes that matter most to us.

15 Minute Pause will inspire and motivate you and stir your soul. Its content is simple yet powerful. Each interactive chapter allows for personal exploration and creativity, with white space to capture your aha moments, reflections, and musings. The playbook will help you to change negative habits into positive rituals. Those who read this book will know what it means to make a long-lasting change for the better, ultimately giving you the tools to shift your perceptions and encourage you to create time for yourself to recharge and re-energize.

[1] *https://www.payscale.com/career-news/2012/08/40-hour-workweek*

15 Minute Pause is divided into three parts:

Introspection
Decision
& Purposeful Action

It is designed to be user-friendly and results focused.

Part One
INTROSPECTION

Focuses on building self-awareness, assessing where you are now, where you want to be, and what obstacles are getting in your way to living your best life. It specifically helps you to identify the emotional, physical and mental stressors and consequences affecting you. These chapters focus on how to overcome the mind chatter and patterns of behavior that keep you stuck. Part One also guides you to create an internal and external support system that will help you stay on track.

Part Two
DECISION

Focuses on what it means to make conscious choices that help you to move forward. You will have the opportunity to take The Life Energy Inventory to assess how you spend your time and where your energy is drained and at its lowest. This will show you which areas of your life are thriving and which areas are suffering and need more attention. Part two guides you to prioritize and make conscious decisions.

Part Three
PURPOSEFUL ACTION

Designed to be dipped into and out of as needed. It is divided into seven chapters that feed your mind, body, heart, your soul purpose, career, creativity and your philanthropic aspirations.

Each chapter has twenty-five suggestions that are insightful, unusual, fun, and engaging. It takes only 15 minutes a day to integrate one of these into your daily life. These ideas are a purposeful nudge to make small, doable changes 15 minutes at a time. This is your 'me time' to experience more energy, to be playful and thoughtful, to reflect, to risk, and to add more joy into your day-to-day life.

i-MATTER EQUATION™

=

Self-Awareness
+
Conscious Choice
+
15 Minute Pause

PART ONE

INTROSPECTION

"Self-awareness is the first step
to change."

CHAPTER ONE
MIRROR MIRROR

Consider this your friendly wake-up call to take a good look at yourself and your life as if you were under a microscope. Sound strange or uncomfortable? When you look closely and realistically at yourself you can make different choices that positively affect the life you are living right now.

As you go through this playbook, you will understand why self-awareness is the first step in the i-Matter Equation and how it's essential on the path to taking time out for yourself. In this chapter, we identify different ways to become more self-aware. We show you what it means to clarify your needs, to pause and notice joyous moments. We provide you with opportunities and activities to be mindful of your thoughts and beliefs, and to be aware of the decisions you make. When you are self-aware, you are better able to recognize what needs to change, what is missing, and what you are grateful for in your day-to-day life.

A busy friend and working mom, who'd been burning her candle at both ends, recently recounted how she sat down with her children in the park on a glorious spring day, where they had encountered a squirrel sunning himself on the path. They all sat cross-legged and watched him for 15 minutes. The seventeen-month-old was fascinated, and the three-year-old was completely mesmerized. This mom was surprised that she was able to simply relax and enjoy the moment with her children. When seen through the eyes of her children, *this pause* brought to her attention how rarely she stopped and noticed what is, literally, in front of her.

How often have you missed similar joyous moments because you were so busy, distracted by your phone, endless to-do's, stressors and constant mind chatter? The point is, as children we savor each day, live minute by minute, and understand joy to be our innate right. As adults, we grow out of this by getting caught up in "stuff," and lose sight of what makes our lives joy-filled. We forget what it means to be present, fearless, carefree and to take precious time for ourselves.

When we are self-aware, we learn to retrain our negative thoughts to create more positive habits like taking "me" time and recognizing joyous moments when they appear, a warm shower, the touch of a loved one, or a delicious cup of tea. Taking time to tune in to ourselves allows our self-awareness to grow— we then take better self-care and can see the joy that surrounds us.

NOTE TO SELF

We've all heard those profound instructions on an airplane: "You have to put the oxygen mask on yourself before your child or anyone else sitting next to you." The truth is, you can't help others if you are not helping yourself first. How many times have we been reminded of this powerful phrase? Yet, we still go about our daily lives focused on everyone and everything except ourselves. *Note to self*--learn to take care of you first, this is the essence of the i-Matter equation. If you don't care for yourself, then you can't truly take care of others.

As our daily stressors increase exponentially, many of us are finding it difficult to take care of our own needs. This imbalance is proving detrimental to our long-term health and well-being. Consider the following as our lifestyle choices are becoming headline news. Increased stress levels are linked to six leading causes of death: heart disease, cancer, lung ailments, accidents, cirrhosis of the liver, and suicide. Furthermore, did you know that 75 percent of Americans experience some sort of physical symptoms related to stress in any given month, and 73 percent experience psychological or mental symptoms [1]? Pause and think about it. Most of us are experiencing stress at such a high level that it is having a negative effect on our health and relationships. Are you?

Consider how you spend your time. When was the last time you thought about how you want your life to be? This may mean taking time-out from your regular routine to spend time doing what you enjoy or with the people who matter most to you.

Professor Mark Williams [2] says, "What we know from neuroscience, from looking at the brain scans of people that are always rushing around, who never taste their food, who are always going from one task to another without actually realizing what they're doing, is that the emotional part of the brain that drives people is on sort of high alert all the time - they're rushing around just as if they were escaping from a predator. But nobody can run fast enough to escape their own worries."

WHERE DO YOU CURRENTLY SPEND YOUR TIME AND ENERGY?

Like many of us, we spend most of our time working and, therefore, most of our time is with colleagues, acquaintances, and associates rather than with our family, friends, and even ourselves. This guide encourages you to carve 15 minutes of precious time for what matters most to you.

How many times have we all heard, *life is short?* This is your time to step up and own your right to have the best life possible. This isn't a Pollyanna perspective (all sunshine and happiness)—rather it acknowledges there are always challenges and obstacles. The only difference is how you choose to manage or respond to them. Recognizing how precious life really is helps us by making it easier to find the meaning, the humor, the lessons, and the opportunities despite the pain and fear. Your ability to cultivate healthy coping mechanisms, to build resilience and strength will eventually bring you more joy and help you move through the challenges. Joy breeds resilience, creativity, and positivity, which leads to more joy.

"

Take a moment for
yourself daily,
if not now,
then when?

"

i-MATTER SCALE

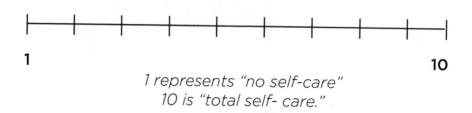

1   **10**

1 represents "no self-care"
10 is "total self- care."

Be honest.
Go with your first response and put an X where you are right now.

Your answer shows whether you need to make a conscious choice to change your present circumstances. If you have marked it below 7, this is your opportunity to help yourself make positive changes. If you marked above 7, consider this a reminder to continue taking time for yourself and to see how you can still improve. The answer given represents this moment in time.

Make sure to check in with yourself regularly to stay on track.

Now that you know where you stand on the i-Matter scale, what are you going to do about it? This book encourages you to notice and carve out time for yourself.

If you are able to practice living a life where you matter, you will learn to:

- Take regular "me" time
- Say no when necessary
- Ask for what you truly want
- Reframe and prioritize
- Be more straightforward
- Value and stand up for yourself
- Be accountable

Are you willing to take care of your needs, at the very least, as much as you care for others? Start by putting yourself on your to-do list.

EYES WIDE SHUT

Let's look at where you are now. Are you walking through life with your eyes shut, doing what you've always done, as if you were on automatic pilot? Or staying in your comfort zone because it's familiar and safe yet not that satisfying? Do you wish you could have more time to yourself, more harmonious relationships, more creativity, or a fulfilling career?

If yes, then take this time to find out where you are now and what you can do to nurture your joy-filled life.

IS LIFE FULL OF DRUDGERY, WORK, OR PLAY?

Take a moment and explore your life from three different perspectives. This is an opportunity to assess how you feel about your life right now and how you would like it to be.
Is life full of drudgery, work or play?

» Think of drudgery as what you don't want to do, (your job, traffic, cleaning the yard, shoveling snow) it's what you typically resist or put off and drains your energy.

» Work is neutral, and it's not something you like or dislike. It doesn't zap or boost your energy. It is what you need to do to take care of daily life (for example, brushing your teeth, getting ready for the day, your job, or aspects of life that need to be done.)

» Finally, play is what you enjoy doing and energizes you (your job, a creative project, a hobby.) It's when you are "in the flow" and suddenly time passes by and you wonder where it went.

PAUSE

Be completely honest as you evaluate where you see yourself in each of these three areas. On the left are three boxes. Give each box a percentage out of 100 to determine how much of your time is spent on drudgery, work or play. The grand total for all three boxes equals 100%. Now reflect on the boxes on the aspirational side and follow the same premise, however, this time imagine how you'd like to spend your time moving forward.

TODAY   ASPIRATION

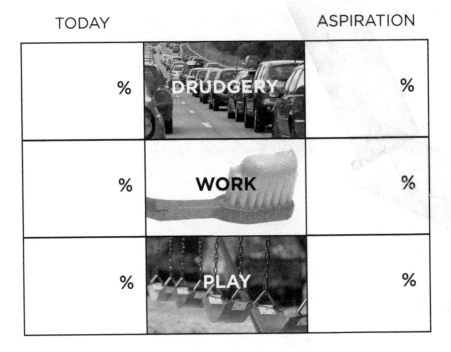

The Drudgery, Work, Play Model is from The Valuable
Office Professional, Michelle Burke 1997.

9

Looking at the results, which area drudgery,
work or play has the lowest score?

Which area has the highest?

Write down what surprised you.

What are you aware of as a result?

You now have some idea of how you live life at present,
and how you wish it could be.

PAUSE

Take a few minutes to think about your life as it stands today. What words would you use to describe it (for example, calm, energized, boring, stressful, overwhelming or hectic)?

1.

2.

3.

4.

5.

REFLECT

Reflect on the words you wrote down. Do the majority represent play? If not, let's find out what is stopping you from having more joy. Consider the stress in your life. List what is draining your energy below. Don't censor yourself, this is the time to be real and honest.

1.

2.

3.

4.

5.

You are not alone, we all have energy drainers that cause stress in our lives. According to the American Psychological Association [3] everyday stressors, boredom, and living in overdrive can reduce your levels of joy. This also decreases productivity on the job and is associated with less harmonious relationships off the job.

After all, in today's fast-paced world, we all struggle to find balance juggling everything we must do. Ironically, we've convinced ourselves that somehow, we can do everything. This is an opportunity to re-evaluate your priorities and mindset and to make choices on how you'd like your life to be right now. We will encourage and guide you throughout this book to find different ways to reduce the drudgery and increase your play percentage in your day-to-day life.

Now take a few minutes and reflect on what energizes you and brings you joy. List as many as you can think of here.

When was the last time you had more play than drudgery in your life?

When we have more play in our lives, it counters the drudgery and helps create a better balance. Furthermore, it helps us to cope with adversity and adds to our quality of life and well-being.

The demands of the fast-paced and unforgiving 24/7 lifestyle and the imbalance that it creates are having far-reaching consequences. We complicate this further by ignoring the warning signs. Remember the statistics that we described earlier. Anxiety, stress, and a lack of joy often stem from the fact that there are simply not enough hours in the day to balance work, home, social life, your children's lives, and everyday tasks. When we don't stop to pause, long enough to re-evaluate or re-prioritize, then the situation naturally becomes worse.

Ironically, most of us believe we are managing our stressors and yet are often unaware of how our actions and moods are negatively impacting us and those closest to us. This point was supported in a recent study when Marcus Buckingham [4], asked a thousand third-through twelfth-graders "If you were granted one wish that would change the way that your mother's work affects your life, what would that wish be?" In a parallel study, the mothers were asked to guess what their children would wish for. Here's what was found: "Most mothers (56 percent) guessed that their children would wish for more time with them. In fact, only ten percent of children made that wish. Their most frequent wish: *'I want my mom to be less stressed and tired' (34 percent).*"

Aren't children perceptive? The fact that children sense when we are stressed and tired, despite our efforts to mask our stresses, is a wake-up call to take better care when managing our lives. We think we are fooling our children, and yet we are really fooling ourselves.

Life is not a practice run; you don't get to relive your twenties, thirties, forties, or fifties again. Take the necessary time now to put your priorities in order and determine how you want to live your life; it's vital to your overall well-being and happiness.

The next chapter asks you to think about your dreams, your goals, and the life you want to create moving forward. We encourage you to dream big and don't hold back.

REFLECTION

The Reflection section is at the end of each chapter and is designed for you to take a pause to reflect upon what you just read. To think about what stands out for you, what you learned, and will take away. Answer the questions honestly for you to get the most from it. You might be surprised by your answers.

1. Where is your current level of self-awareness on a scale of 1 to 10 (1 being none and 10 being highly self-aware)?

2. In terms of your to-do list, what is not a real priority?

3. What will you do differently to add to your percentage of play?

[1] *Stress in America, Our Health at Risk, 2012, American Psychological Association (APA).*
[2] *"Mindfulness: Finding Peace in a Frantic World" Professor Mark Williams*
[3] *American Psychological Association, Stress in America, Our Health at Risk, 2012*
[4] *Women's Happiness What We Know for Certain, Marcus Buckingham, Huffington Post Sept 2009*

"

Joy-filled moments
don't add more to
an already busy day,
rather they make the
busy day better.

"

CHAPTER TWO
DREAM BIG

We have just discovered where your life is at present, and now it's time to focus on how you want your life to be. The good news is you get to decide on how you want to live it. Dream big, and don't limit yourself. Living your best life is different for everybody. For one person, it might mean traveling around the world to experience a different culture, or raising a family of smart, loving kids, finding a loving partner, or maybe it means getting a business off the ground, being philanthropic or getting involved in humanitarian causes. Martin Luther King, famous for his "I Have a Dream" speech, inspired a nation. Do the same for yourself.

As children, we've all had a dream and as time goes by, we often put our dream on a shelf because it didn't seem possible or someone came along and squashed it. Maybe now is the time to dream up a new dream by asking, "What do you want your life to be?" Think about what you value, what's important to you. This will help you determine your big dream or resurrect a dream from the past. What's important is declaring your dream out loud and taking steps to making it a reality.

Following are activities to help you move in the direction you desire. When you increase your awareness and determine your values, then you can take appropriate action to achieve what you really want. Uncover what has true meaning for you through the values activity on the following page.

YOUR VALUES
GUIDE YOUR DREAMS

Your values make you who you are.

They guide you to be true to yourself.

If your choices are aligned with your values, life becomes easier and can bring more joy.

Values are personal to you and only you decide what is important when it comes to being true to yourself.

For example, is it necessary to live with integrity, have growth and learning in your life, self-expression, create intimate relationships, be financially secure, independent, or philanthropic?

FIND A QUIET MOMENT

Consider who you are without all the baggage, the duties, the roles, and the expectations. Most importantly, do you like the person you see and the life you are leading now?

What really matters most to you in your heart of hearts? Close your eyes and imagine how you'd be feeling. Would you be calmer, laughing, feeling energized, or more content? What would you be doing? Spending time with those who really matter, traveling, or learning? Write down your top five values. Your values define what matters most to you, and what you live your life by. Think of these as your "must haves" to living your best life. Write your answers below.

a) e.g. Self-Expression/Following a Passion
b) e.g. Intimacy/Compassion/Nurturing

1.

2.

3.

4.

5.

Are these values showing up in your life at present? If so how? If not what's getting in the way? Be specific.

Living a conscious and authentic lifestyle means living life according to your values instead of drifting through life on autopilot as most of us do. Each of us has our own set of values. These values impact the choices we make and influence the way we take care of ourselves.

PROPEL YOURSELF INTO THE FUTURE

Imagine you are 80 years old looking back on your life. Would you be happy with the way you lived your life?

What is your legacy? Write your answers here and then think about how you can make changes now to have the life you want.

Have you noticed that as you get older, time seems to accelerate, and the years seem to get shorter? The list of promises get longer, shelved, or relegated to "I'll do that when I have more time or money." Yet years later, you are still waiting to fulfill those promises. This playbook is your opportunity to act now. Lilamani had her aha moment about twenty years ago. She was enjoying her job and traveling. She was lucky enough to visit some far away locations, where she was involved in filming everything from grizzly bears to orangutans and killer whales. A dream job in many ways, and one she worked hard to achieve.

However, dreams and goals change, and for her, the clues became increasingly obvious. The small voice inside her head was dissatisfied and told her things weren't quite right. She had visions of working for herself, free of nine to five constraints, with the desire to do something of value. Her needs included a better quality of life, with more time for herself and time with family (in New Zealand). The thought of leaving what was secure to go and do something that was uncertain, was daunting. In her mind it meant she had greater scope to experiment and try new things. She had a belief that as she continued to do what was meaningful to her, the money would follow.

She took a leap of faith and although scary, the relief was almost palpable when she finally made the decision. The journey has had its twists and turns, but nothing can take away from following her heart. She learned that failure is nothing to be ashamed of and in fact, it is a big part of life that teaches important lessons. She knows that when money is short, it can be earned whether it's $10 or $50 an hour. More importantly, she doesn't need as much stuff and learned less is more. Her expenses are lower and the time she spent doing odd projects are now spent on our co-founded business. Her greatest reward - the courage to follow her dream and see it coming to fruition.

How do you want your life to be now?

On the following two pages, put your dreams down in writing, a drawing or glue some pictures to visualize what you want for your life. Be bold and make it specific. Revisit the pages to remind yourself of what you want. Believe it's possible.

START LIVING
YOUR DREAM NOW

You don't have to wait.

What do you need to do to put this dream into motion?
Take 15 minutes now and think about what steps you can take this
week. Write them here:

1.

2.

3.

4.

5.

REFRAME

The question isn't how to add more to your already busy life and packed to-do list. Instead, it's about reframing and thinking of your life in terms of quality rather than quantity. It's your right to take a pause. When you take this time-out to assess what you no longer want, you hone in on what you do want, your dreams, goals and aspirations.

We encourage you to live your dream by finding, creating, and pouring in the joyous moments, living your dream doesn't mean escaping the difficulties and challenges; rather, it requires that you learn to build in the pauses, the moments of fun, compassion, joy, and passion no matter what unexpected and difficult experiences you may endure. That is what makes for a kinder and more fulfilled life.

The next chapter will help you to understand what obstacles can get in the way of living your dream. We encourage you to rein in your critical and negative thoughts and foster an awareness of your mental triggers. Knowing how your mindset affects your day-to-day decisions and your capacity to live a joyous life is essential. When you change your negative thoughts, you change your life for the better.

REFLECTION

Was there anything that surprised you about your dreams?

What was the greatest takeaway from this chapter?

What is one action you will take to start fulfilling your dream?

Who will you share your dream with that will support you in bringing it to life? Write their name(s) here and commit to asking them for support.

"

It all begins and ends in your mind. What you give power to has power over you if you allow it.

"

CHAPTER THREE
THE WAY YOU THINK IS THE WAY YOU ACT

Over the next three chapters, you will have the opportunity to
assess your mental, physical and emotional well-being. These three
areas are intimately integrated. We will show you, when one area
is overly stressed, it impacts the other areas. Also, we provide
tips, tools and strategies on how to manage these stressors.

While we were writing this, we found a study on stress and gender,
which showed that the number one barrier to making a change
for women is the lack of willpower. When asked what they would
need to change for their willpower to improve, women were
more likely than men to say less fatigue and more energy [1].

Given these results, we wanted to find out the reasons for the
various causes of your fatigue. We look at your mental, physical
and emotional triggers and responses. This will give you a better
understanding of the price you are paying and ultimately help
increase your energy levels, so you can make positive change.

MENTAL ENERGY

Mental Energy refers to the ability to be
aware of your thoughts, to stimulate the mind
in positive ways, gain knowledge, improve
a skill, and promote a healthy mindset.

MIND CONTROL

This chapter explores how your negative thoughts keep you stuck. It helps you become more aware of your thoughts and the influence they have on your well-being. Specifically, we focus on how to change your negative mindset.

Our mind is a powerful and dynamic tool. The thoughts we have in our head make the difference between how joy-filled or fearful we are. You are accountable for the thoughts you choose to focus on, so make them positive. Consider what life has to offer: friendship, love, passionate endeavors, books, art, purposeful work, music, nature; the list is endless. The only difference is how we perceive it. Have you wondered what gets in the way? We believe the way you think is the way you act.

While exploring the subject, we found that negativity breeds fear, and fear breeds negativity. This can go on to foster other negative emotions like increased anxiety, resistance, procrastination, anger or blame, all of which keep us stuck. Evidence shows [1], those who have more control over their negative emotions are more likely to be optimistic and have greater life satisfaction, health and well-being. When you focus your thoughts to be more positive, those feelings create social connectedness, perceived social support, and serve as a more productive coping response. Thereby, positive people are more likely to be happy. They live longer and enjoy a better quality of life.

This begs the question, are you willing to shift your thinking, lighten your "negative load," and break old mental habits that no longer serve you?

We refer to the internal voices in our heads as the negative Meddler*
and the positive Player*. Most of us recognize the Meddler as a
masterful sabotager who creates excuses and barriers to keep us from
doing what is right and best for us. The Meddler voice is a whiner; it
constantly complains about what is wrong in the world and increases
our anxieties, doubts, and fears. This Meddler voice is your nemesis
because it really knows how to spin a story of excuses about why
we can't do what we love, why we shouldn't pursue a dream, or why
we aren't allowed to take time for ourselves; and the list goes on.
The Player voice is your cheerleader, friend, coach, and avid
supporter. Its goal is to acknowledge you and empower
you to step up, inspire you to take time for yourself,
and help you to embrace joyous moments daily.

Those of us who are overly busy, frantic and stressed may not
notice the Meddler voice. The negative Meddler creeps in when
we allow the pace of life and lack of time to override our sense
of wonder and joy. Imagine you find yourself with a hectic week
ahead, and the tasks keep piling up. You cancel your night out with
friends, your gym session, and eat lunch on the run. The perception
that we must do everything but give ourselves time to pause is
the Meddler in sabotage mode. When multitasking becomes a
competitive sport, the negativity is more likely to gradually sneak in.

STOP RIGHT NOW AND NOTICE YOUR INTERNAL VOICE.

Pause for a full minute. What is going through your mind in this moment? Is your mind chatter irritable, overly analytical, annoyed, frustrated, or is it cheerful, encouraging and positive? Write down or draw a picture of your thoughts. Don't censor yourself; write it all down. It's common to have negative, disorganized, and random thoughts flying through your brain. The only way to make a positive conscious choice is to be aware of what thoughts are consuming your mind. Be honest with yourself.

A study in the journal Cognitive Therapy and Research found that functional groups (those with a happier mindset) have at least 1.7 positive thoughts to every negative thought. Whereas, mildly dysfunctional groups have a ratio of one positive to one negative thought. This intriguing research shows that the more negative thoughts we have, the greater the mental dysfunction, whereas, those who have at least two positive thoughts for each negative are likely to be happier [2].

Negative mind chatter can be destructive to our self-confidence. The fear we carry and the obstacles we encounter differ from person to person. They appear in numerous shapes and guises. You will recognize them as the naysayer, unhelpful patterns of destructive behavior, time-consuming excuses and energy drainers. These negative influences are unforgiving, sarcastic, and quick to criticize. Consider these your red flags.

To overcome the negative influences, we need to learn how to acknowledge the Meddler without giving it control. The Meddler loves a pessimist. The Player voice, on the other hand, has the capacity to turn negative experiences into a learning opportunity, a blessing in disguise or simply to accept them and move on. Optimists can look on the bright side and that gives them an edge. This is supported by numerous studies that encourage mindfulness as a tool to first become aware and then manage our thoughts. Positive thinking creates space to pause, allowing us to breakout of habitual ineffective patterns [3]. By cultivating a positive Player mindset, we diminish the Meddler's power and make better choices.

When you notice the Meddler rearing its ugly head, tune in and listen more closely to the internal "Player voice", your friendly cheerleader, who is always present. The Player's voice often goes unheard when the Meddler's voice is loud and persistent. Learn to recognize which internal voice is dominant. The more aware you are, the better you become at identifying which voice is leading you, and the better you become at making conscious choices that benefit you. This is about mastering your mind, in the same way as you choose what clothes you wear each day, you have the power to choose your thoughts.

PAUSE

Read each of the statements in both columns and check all those that dominate your mind in either the Meddler or Player column. We encourage you to add other statements that are dominating your mindset. The more honest and clear you are about the messages inside your head, the better able you are to make changes.

√	MEDDLER	PLAYER	√
	I WAKE UP DURING THE NIGHT BECAUSE OF MY MIND CHATTER	I SLEEP WELL THROUGH THE NIGHT	
	TOO MANY PEOPLE ARE COUNTING ON ME	I HELP MYSELF FIRST AND THEN I FIND THE ENERGY TO HELP OTHERS	
	I WOULD FEEL TOO GUILTY	I REWARD MYSELF AND DO THE THINGS THAT BRING ME JOY	
	I CAN'T STOP	I TAKE TIME TO RELAX DAILY	
	I CAN'T SEE HOW THIS WILL HELP ME	THIS MAKES A POSITIVE DIFFERENCE FOR ME AND MY FAMILY	
	I AM BEING SELFISH	I DO WHAT IS ESSENTIAL FOR MY WELL-BEING	
	I AM TOO STRESSED WITH TOO MUCH TO DO ALREADY	IT'S OKAY NOT TO DO EVERYTHING ON MY TO-DO LIST TODAY	
	I CAN'T BECAUSE I AM TOO BUSY	IT'S OK TO FIND TIME FOR MYSELF	

√	MEDDLER	PLAYER	√
	I'LL DO IT MYSELF, BECAUSE NO ONE ELSE CAN DO IT AS WELL AS I CAN	IT'S OKAY TO DELEGATE	
	I CAN'T FIND TIME AS OTHERS NEED ME	I AM EQUALLY IMPORTANT	
	I DON'T HAVE THE MONEY OR RESOURCES	I HAVE FUN WITHOUT SPENDING A LOT OF MONEY	
	I DO IT ALL BECAUSE I DON'T HAVE EXTRA HELP	I ASK FOR HELP	
	I AM TOO TIRED	I FEEL REVIVED IF I TAKE TIME FOR ME	
	ADD YOUR OWN STATEMENTS BELOW:		

| | TOTAL MEDDLER STATEMENTS | TOTAL PLAYER STATEMENTS | |

How many did you check off in the Meddler column and how many in the Player column?

Which one was dominant?

If you have more checked off on the right, the Player's column, it means your positive thoughts are fully activated. Continue to focus on the Player who helps you to forgive, brings you joy, self-care, and balance and ultimately supports your i-Matter Equation. If you have more statements on the left side, the Meddler is ruling your thoughts. These negative thoughts drain your mental energy and are a waste of time. They prevent you from moving forward and reaching your joy potential.

Remind yourself that the Meddler does not have your best interests at heart. The Meddler's goal is to create barriers and unrealistic expectations that set you up to fail. So, when you find yourself in negative mode know the Meddler is speaking loudly. Worse still, the shocking news is the person who is doing this to you is often the person you see in the mirror every day.

KEEPING THE MEDDLER IN CHECK

Stop self-destructive behavior and continue to monitor your negative self- talk. A powerful way to do this is to observe how often the destructive Meddler and supportive Player show up in your day-to-day life.

Track your thoughts by putting a rubber band on your wrist, and each time you notice a negative, critical, sarcastic, fearful, doubting thought, snap the rubber band. This is a reminder to retrain your thoughts by turning around a negative attitude and reframing it as a lesson or opportunity. Notice how often this happens throughout the day. This will build your self-awareness and give you the power and confidence to quiet the Meddler voice and replace with the positive Player's voice. Research tells us that when we do this every day for twenty-one days consecutively, it literally changes the neural pathways in our brain, which allows us to create a new, positive habit. Start today by marking it on your calendar.

Another option is to practice mindfulness meditation. It eases stress and anxiety. New research, according to Carolyn Schatz, the editor of the Harvard Health Letter [4], shows that mindfulness meditation changes the way nerves connect, helping to ease physical and psychological problems, from high blood pressure and chronic pain to anxiety and binge eating.

We found that even the smallest of things can turn our negative thoughts around, such as a smile from a stranger, having no traffic on the way home from work, or an unexpected call from a friend. Our personal experiences have shown us that if we want to break an unhealthy lifestyle choice or habit, some type of shift is required—a shift in perspective and mindset. How you choose to see your life, and the thoughts you choose to have can make life either joyful or joyless.

Michelle had been taking meditation classes and practicing on and off for years, however, had not cultivated a true practice until three years ago after her father unexpectedly passed away. She was struggling and needed something to help her cope and shift her negative thoughts, so she decided to attend a Deepak Chopra three-day meditation retreat. Michelle was reminded of the value of meditating and gained immediate results. She felt calmer, present and she could hear more of the Player voice again. This experience helped her put this mindful meditation into a practice and now she meditates for 15 minutes daily. She is currently taking mindfulness classes at UCLA to keep her practice alive.

In the next chapter, we will help you to tune into your positive Player voice, your friend and cheerleader. We show you how to make conscious decisions to pause, reframe, and focus the positive aspects of life.

*Meddler and Player referenced from The Valuable OfficeProfessional, 1997 by Michelle Burke

[1]Happy People Live Longer: Subjective Well-Being Contributes to Health and Longevity, (IAAP) Ed Diener University of Illinois and the Gallup Organization, USA and Micaela Y. Chan University of Texas, Dallas 2011

[2] "Mindfulness: Finding Peace in a Frantic World" Professor Mark Williams https://www.youtube.com/watch?v=0wBZjb8u95o, 2017

[3]http://mindworks.org/blog/how-does-meditation-reduce-stress/2017

[4]Caroline Schatz, Harvard Health Letter, Harvard Women's Healthwatch Harvard Health Publications 2012

REFLECTION

How dominant is the Meddler? Is it increasing or decreasing as time
goes on?

What did you learn about the Meddler in your head?

What will you do to minimize the Meddler's negative mind chatter?

What did you notice that was joyful today?

"

So, the Meddler thinks it can keep your mind trapped in this negative spiral.

Think again.

"

CHAPTER FOUR
CUP HALF FULL

We are all entitled to live our best life; not just exist, but rather truly be fully engaged. A life that is joy filled isn't limited to the lucky few, the wealthy or the famous, it's available to all of us.

It starts with finding the positive Player within. The Player sees life from the cup half full and comments, *I matter. How beautiful. That's pure joy. How thoughtful. How kind.* The Player is grateful, appreciative, notices the beauty in life, and sees random acts of kindness. Tuning into the Player requires paying close attention to the quieter voice, the voice that says, "yes" to you, is kind to you and guides you to pause for 15 minutes each day. Self-care is a choice and the choice is yours.

There are many ways in which to refill your cup. When was the last time you stopped and daydreamed, took time out for lunch, basked in the sun, appreciated a conversation with a child or friend, forgave yourself for a mistake you made, or enjoyed dessert without guilt? The more delight you take in small pleasures, the less exhaustion you will carry.

By paying more attention to the Player, you give yourself permission to feel good which will naturally lead to better self-care. Kindness or gratitude is the quickest and easiest way to keep the Player voice in motion and your cup full.

PAUSE

Notice the Player voice in your head by practicing being
kind to yourself and others. Start by writing down three
each day. Read your list before you go to bed every night
and each morning. This will keep the Player voice alive
and thriving. (e.g., Don't send the mean tweet, let someone
in while driving in traffic, buy flowers for yourself).
Write down three kind acts you experienced
or what you are grateful for.

1.

2.

3.

To continue to maintain and maximize the positive Player's voice, be mindful of how quickly the Meddler, our inner critic, shows up to stop you or derail you from enjoying your life. This is the time to be hyper-vigilant and to listen to the Player's voice. There are many ways to help shift a mood, inspire or energize. Try listening to music you love. Researchers at McGill University in Canada [1] have shown that intense pleasure in listening to music triggered the release of the feel-good chemical, dopamine. Which can change mood and reduce stress levels. Pick a song that transforms your thinking and sing it whenever the Meddler rears its ugly head.

Stay tuned into the Player voice. It will help you to weed out what is and isn't important on your "to do's and should do's". Remember that you aren't just a spouse, parent, sibling, employee, or friend. You are also an individual, who matters. Start by putting yourself at the top of your list by taking time out for yourself each day.

As you listen more often to the Player voice within, you will learn to manage your expectations and be kinder to yourself. The point is you hold the power to approach life and face your challenges in either a positive or a negative way. Your main limitation is the control you give the negative Meddler.

The last two chapters have shown you how the Meddler and Player affect and influence your mental thoughts and actions. This increased awareness will help when it comes to creating your i-Matter Equation at the end of this playbook. In chapter five, you will have the opportunity to diagnose how your emotional stressors and triggers affect self-care, well-being and the capacity for joy.

[1] *Nature Neuroscience Volume:14, 2013, online publication by V N Salimpoor, M Benovoy, K Larcher, A Dagher & RJ Zatorre Anatomically distinct dopamine release during anticipation and experience of peak emotion to music*

REFLECTION

How will you increase the Player's presence in your life?

What can you say to start your day with a Player mindset, for
example, "Today is a great day!"

How did you practice being kinder to yourself and others today?

Did you have an "aha" moment when reading this chapter? If so, what
was it?

WHO'S IN CONTROL OF YOUR THOUGHTS TODAY?

The Meddler or The Player?

the **Meddler**   *the* **Player**

To help you commit to the Player mindset, we have created the Player's Mantra below. These positive affirmations will remind you to value who you are, to enjoy the changes you are making, and to appreciate the life you are living. Practice saying one or all throughout your day. See how it changes your life for the better. We've also added space for you to make up your own.

The Player Mantra

1. I am _____ (e.g joyful, light, loving, grateful)

2. I see joy around me.

3. I feel_____ (e.g my feet
   on the ground, strong, loved)

4. I make healthy decisions that are in my best interest.

5.

The Player's Mantra is a useful tool. Say them out loud and often. They will keep the positive Player in motion and the Meddler at bay. Be wary of the emotionally draining complainer who will creep up on you when you are tired, stressed or de-energized. Allow it to be easy for yourself because you are worthy of living a joy-filled life.

"

You have the
will and the
power to be
emotionally
resilient.

"

EMOTIONAL ENERGY

Emotional Energy refers to the ability to perceive, assess and manage your feelings and emotions, as well as recognize other people's feelings and to respond in a healthy way.

CHAPTER FIVE
EMOTIONAL SHIFT

How often does the logical side of your brain dominate your feelings, emotions, and instincts? This chapter focuses on the emotional rather than the analytical side of you. Let us differentiate these ideas further. Your Intelligence Quotient (IQ) is how quickly you absorb new information and is associated with the power of reason. Emotional Intelligence Quotient (EQ), a term coined by author Daniel Goleman, is a yardstick for measuring social and emotional awareness. It accounts for the joyous highs you experience, your tears and fears, the empathy you have when you step into someone else's shoes, your racing heart when you see someone you love, and your gut instinct when you feel something is wrong.

We explore how you can get in tune with your feelings. Moreover, we show you how your negative emotions affect your ability to live a more joyous life.

Lilamani recalls an interesting conversation with a friend, Jackie, who had described why she would never go to bed angry.

The first argument is the hardest because it feels like the end of the world. Nothing hurts like a broken heart. Jackie recalled how she reacted badly to an insignificant point during a conversation with her partner. How quickly it went from a misunderstanding to anger, hurt, and from there it escalated further. They both said things they wished they hadn't by bringing up irrelevant facts from the past. She left in a huff only to feel alone and regretful. Jackie spent the night tossing and turning, imagining everything was over and wished she hadn't overreacted. The next day was an emotional roller coaster because there was no communication for over 24 hours. They finally talked calmly and resolved their miscommunication. Jackie learned how to better handle this type of situation by recognizing her triggers and not letting them get the best of her. Her new approach is to take a deep breath, pause, change the topic or reframe her thoughts and without exception find a way to come to a mutual understanding.

Jackie and her partner have since married and have made this agreement - not to go to bed arguing. That means, they either agree to disagree, apologize, or forgive and forget. The purpose is to stay true to their promise to make up before they go to bed. And with that comes other benefits too.

We've all been in Jackie's shoes. How have you handled a similar situation? All feelings and emotions are valid. It is what makes us human. This is not about never having negative feelings; it is about managing your feelings. If you are constantly in reactive mode, getting mad, irritated, annoyed, or frustrated by what someone else is saying or doing, then the Meddler is getting the best of you. Thereby, making it increasingly difficult to experience the joyous moments. In addition, for those who bottle their emotions up or ignore them, you risk intensifying your feelings further by expressing them in unhealthy ways like losing your temper or getting ill.

If you know your feelings are getting in the way of having harmonious and healthy relationships or stopping you from keeping a job or living life with more self-care, then you need to examine how to make a positive emotional shift. When we are emotionally perceptive, we tap more often into our positive feelings to improve, manage, and reduce our emotional stressors. When we are accountable for our feelings and emotions, we gain more control, manage our reactions, and make better decisions.

With that in mind, take this opportunity to understand your triggers and how they impact your emotional well-being. In the same way, as we recognize the impact of the negative Meddler on our thought patterns, we need to pay equal attention to what triggers our unhealthy emotions and destructive behavior.

PAUSE

Below is a list of energy zappers that can drain you emotionally. Read each statements and check off any that apply to you today. Be honest with yourself. The more aware you are of your feelings and how they impact your decision making and actions, the less reactive you will be.

☐ When I don't speak up or stand up for myself, I feel less valued.

☐ I feel stressed because I can't keep up with life's demands and expectations.

☐ When I make mistakes, I typically criticize myself and feel bad.

☐ I tend to avoid confrontations because they make me anxious and uncomfortable.

☐ I generally feel nervous when I first meet someone.

☐ When making decisions, I tend to rely on others' opinions because I don't trust my gut instinct.

☐ When I get upset, I take my anger out on the people closest to me.

☐ I feel disconnected from family and friends.

☐ I compare myself to others when I feel insecure.

☐ I feel depressed with how my life is going.

☐ I am hesitant to show my feelings for fear of being hurt.

☐ I am on the defensive a lot of the time.

☐ I let other people's sour moods and
comments affect me negatively.

☐ I feel the need to be perfect to be truly loved or accepted.

☐ I avoid trying anything new because I'm afraid I will fail.

Now, take a closer look at each of the statements that you checked. Let's dig a little deeper, what do you think is the underlying reason for your feelings? Whether its because you've been working long hours, unappreciated by your partner, out of work, or in a conflict with your friend, it's vital to understand the why behind your feelings. When you do, then you can start to manage or shift your emotions when you recognize it showing up.

If you find that you are feeling stuck with continued negative emotions and unable to move forward in a healthy way, then it might be a good time to reach out and speak with someone. Furthermore, if you are unable to stop reacting negatively, feel depressed for an extended time or are harboring strong negative feelings about yourself or others, then seek a trained counselor, therapist, or coach to help you. Reaching out for professional support is a sign of strength, so get the help you need now.

The negative emotional rollercoaster is exhausting, and yet some of us willingly stay there. How can we build emotional resilience, and strength to achieve a better balance? Let's begin by identifying what triggers (internal or external) you react to and put in place solutions to tackle these when they appear.

PAUSE

Take this opportunity to understand your triggers and how they impact your emotional well-being. In the same way, as we recognize the impact of the negative Meddler on our thought patterns, we need to pay equal attention to what triggers our unhealthy emotions and destructive behavior.

What feelings do you have right now? Is it anxiety, joy, fear, frustration, or calm?

Review the Meddler negative emotions list on the following pages and check all those that you've experienced repeatedly in the past 30 days. Move across to the triggers column and describe as specifically as possible what or who caused you to feel this way. For example, an overreaction to your spouse, tiredness, or a heavy work schedule.

Look at your answers and ask yourself if these are keeping you stuck?

What solutions can you put in place to empower yourself to move forward? Write them in the Solutions column (e.g. get a coach, shift your attitude, rethink your priorities or take a 15 minute walk).

MEDDLER'S NEGATIVE EMOTION	INTERNAL & EXTERNAL TRIGGERS	SOLUTIONS
ANXIOUS		
TEARFUL		
LONELY		
WORRIED		
WEARY		
IRRITABLE		
DEPRESSED		
UNHAPPY		
SAD		
SELF-LOATHING		
WHINING		
BORED		

MEDDLER'S NEGATIVE EMOTION	INTERNAL & EXTERNAL TRIGGERS	SOLUTIONS
FRUSTRATED		
ANGRY		
SHORT-TEMPERED		
FEARFUL		
NERVOUS		
JEALOUS		
TENSE		
MOODY		
		ADD YOUR OWN BELOW

If you are experiencing any of these negative emotional symptoms on a consistent basis, seek professional help.

1. Have you noticed any patterns?

2. Is there a person who continues to push your buttons or a situation that is reoccurring?

These negative triggers are responsible for your increased stress levels.

Notice what makes you emotionally reactive and remember you are ultimately accountable for your behavior. You have the willpower to react in a healthy way to people and situations.

NOTICE THE POSITIVE TRIGGERS

Review the list on the following pages and circle all the positive emotions that you've been repeatedly experiencing in the past 30 days. Describe what you believe is the trigger (the cause) in either the internal or external column. For example: if you are feeling peaceful or calm is it because you meditated (internal) or you received a compliment from your manager about your work and are feeling happy (external)? Write down in the discovery column what you noticed or learned about yourself in regards to the positive trigger; for example: felt accepted or stimulated.

PLAYER'S POSITIVE EMOTION	INTERNAL OR EXTERNAL TRIGGERS	DISCOVERY
CONFIDENT		
PEACEFUL		
CURIOUS		
GRATEFUL		
ENTHUSIASTIC		
PASSIONATE		
BUOYANT		
LOVING		
LIGHT-HEARTED		
PLAYFUL		
ENERGETIC		
GRACIOUS		

PLAYER'S POSITIVE EMOTION	INTERNAL OR EXTERNAL TRIGGERS	DISCOVERY
HAPPY		
CALM		
CENTERED		
OPTIMISTIC		
RELAXED		
COURAGEOUS		
INSPIRED		
JOYFUL		
		ADD YOUR OWN BELOW

TIPS FOR MANAGING YOUR NEGATIVE TRIGGERS

1. Feel your feet on the ground, wiggle your toes right now, and feel the ground before responding.

2. Breathe and practice counting to twenty before you say anything.

3. Pause for 15 minutes and walk away from the situation until you are calmer and able to discuss it in a responsible manner.

Another recommendation for being less reactive is from 'A Woman's Health', which shows journaling for 15 minutes a day is key in lowering stress and reducing negative emotions. [1]. This evidence is supported by Dr. James Pennebaker, [2] a pioneer in social psychology who conducted a study in 1986, asking participants to write down their traumatic life events for 15 minutes at a time. He found that those who did had fewer visits to the health center. He concluded that keeping emotions a secret led to increasing health problems, while disclosing thoughts and feelings led to better health.

Continue to monitor when and how you react to the various triggers. Stay the course.

These past two chapters focused on your mental and emotional well-being. You examined the various emotional obstacles, mental barriers, excuses, triggers, and drainers that hamper your progress. In the next chapter, we explore your physical health and well-being.

[1]http://awomanshealth.com/journal-for-stress-relief/

[2]Pennebaker, J.W. & Beall, S.K. (1986). Confronting a traumatic event: Toward an understanding of inhibition and disease. Journal of Abnormal Psychology, 95, 274-281.

REFLECTION

What is one aha moment you can take away from this chapter?

How will you manage your emotions better so that you stop going into reactive mode?

Did you have a moment when you felt grateful today? What was it for?

Name one person who could benefit from learning this and share it with them.

"

The body
doesn't lie; it is
your internal
barometer.

"

PHYSICAL ENERGY

Physical Energy refers to the awareness of how
your whole body feels; it is the momentum
for taking good care of your body, your timely
response to addressing pain and the action
you take to have overall physical wellness.

CHAPTER SIX
PHYSICAL CHECK-UP

How many nights do you spend tossing and turning, or experience your heart racing? Are you short of breath or having difficulty relaxing? Is your stomach in knots and are headaches more frequent? According to WebMD, you are not alone; 75-90% of all doctor's office visits are for stress-related ailments and complaints. Stress can play a part in problems such as headaches, high blood pressure, heart problems, skin conditions, asthma, arthritis, diabetes, depression, and anxiety [1].

We believe that physical stressors are a direct result of the lifestyle we lead. We seem to have lost sight of what has real meaning and joy often because of our all-consuming duties, responsibilities, and endless to-do's. Let's be realistic, nobody is going to be able to erase life's stressors completely, in fact some stress is beneficial. It can help us to move forward and motivate us. The challenge is paying attention to when the stress becomes too much and has a negative impact.

When stress is overwhelming, it can escalate to chronic stress. According to a recent survey by Stress in America, "If stress becomes chronic, it can lead to significant health consequences. It's important to remember that there are steps that people can take to manage their stress in healthy and productive ways, like exercising, spending time with friends and family and finding ways to get involved in your community."

Without proper management of stress levels, we are often too tired and fatigued to function in a productive way. Are you drained and experiencing adverse physical symptoms due to your stress?

Both of us have struggled with chronic stress and because we ignored it, negative physical symptoms appeared. Increased awareness and better decision making have taught us how to manage our stressors.

Michelle had a serious health scare in her 30's because she didn't heed the initial signs of weight loss and extreme tiredness. Michelle was "too busy" managing her consulting company, traveling and working with clients. The final straw came when her symptoms became worse, losing more weight, sweating uncontrollably and her voice changed.

After visiting her doctor and getting an MRI, she learned there were two large masses growing, one in her thyroid and the other in her esophagus. Doctors were convinced it was thyroid cancer. Her surgery was successful, and was diagnosed with hyperthyroidism, a common ailment for women in their 30's and 40's. If left untreated, it would have life threatening consequences. This was her wake-up call. Today, Michelle takes a daily thyroid pill and is very grateful it wasn't cancer. She now pays closer attention to the early signs and practices taking a pause every day.

Michelle learned a valuable lesson - to listen to her body and to the stressors before they escalate and to take action. She is thankful that she took notice of the final red flag and is here to share her story with you. Today, Michelle travels only one week out of the month, takes devoted fun time for herself, has a daily gratitude practice and takes daily walks with her dog, Roxie.

The greater point for all of us - stress is not an illness; rather it causes serious illness. If we ignore the signs, and do not learn to recognize the triggers or the physical symptoms early, we risk our health. The triggers we experience are unique to each of us and can include anything from long, exhausting workdays, to taking care of a baby, anxiety over financial burdens, struggling with insecurities, or juggling kids and work. Whatever the challenge, we need to pay closer attention to the symptoms because these are considered our "red flags."

PHYSICAL WELL-BEING DIAGNOSTIC QUIZ

Stop in this moment and listen to what your body is telling you. How is your body feeling? Does your neck hurt? Are you feeling sluggish, tired, having heart palpitations?

We identified a list of the most common physical symptoms.

Read through and check all the symptoms you are currently experiencing. Identify the triggers that are causing these symptoms. Think about what you were doing, and who you were with to uncover any patterns. For example, your stomach is in knots, you rate your stress level at 8 because you had an unresolved fight with your spouse. Rate your level of stress between 1 (very little stress) and 10 (highly stressed). Be honest as the results are vital to increasing self-awareness and well-being.

If you are experiencing any of these symptoms on a regular basis, be sure to consult with your doctor.

PHYSICAL SYMPTOM	STRESS RATING 1-10	WHAT IS THE TRIGGER? WHAT WERE YOU DOING? WHO WITH?
STOMACHACHE, STOMACH IN KNOTS		
INCREASED FATIGUE OR SLEEPING LONGER HOURS, OR UNABLE TO GET OUT OF BED		
HEAD, NECK OR BACKACHE		
CRYING UNCONTROLLABLY		
CHANGE IN APPETITE, OVER OR UNDER EATING		
CHANGE IN SEX DRIVE		
GRINDING TEETH		
INDIGESTION		
CONTINUOUS ITCHING		
INCREASED USE OF ALCOHOL, DRUGS, OR CIGARETTES		
INABILITY TO CONCENTRATE OR FOCUS		

PHYSICAL SYMPTOM	STRESS RATING 1-10	WHAT IS THE TRIGGER? WHAT WERE YOU DOING? WHO WITH?
NAIL BITING REGULARLY		
INCREASED SWEATING		
TOSSING OR TURNING, INTERRUPTED SLEEP		
LACK OF ENERGY I.E. LETHARGIC		
MORE THAN 2-3 PROLONGED COLDS, FLUS, OR SORE THROATS PER YEAR		
CONSTIPATION OR DIARRHEA		
ULCERS		
HEART PALPITATIONS		
NAUSEA OR DIZZINESS		
MUSCLE TENSION		
CONSTANT PACING AND UNABLE TO STAND STILL		
INABILITY TO RELAX		

1. Did you notice any patterns for the various triggers and stressors you checked? Is the same situation happening repeatedly? If you find it is caused by a situation or person, what can you do about it?

2. How often are you experiencing the physical symptoms checked above: daily, weekly, monthly, or once in a while? It is critical to be honest, as these symptoms can have an immediate impact on your health, and you might need to consult a medical professional.

Congratulations for being honest with yourself and acknowledging what is really going on in your body. The point is, you get to choose how you want to move forward, manage your stress, and improve your well-being.

Given our own health issues, we, too, had to make some changes. Today, we pay closer attention and pause for 15 minutes or more every day, reassess, and practice listening to how our body is feeling. We take the necessary time-outs when we feel overly tired, sick, or drained. This has helped us to manage our stressors and notice more joy.

The last three chapters showed how the mind, body and emotions are intimately integrated. We identified that your mental health affects your emotional health, which in turn affects your physical health and how this directly influences your overall well-being. Ultimately, if any one of these areas is depleted it has the potential to affect the others so influencing your lifestyle and capacity for joy. As the Roman poet Juvenal pointed out as far back as the 1st Century, Menes Sana in Corpora Sano "You should pray for a healthy mind in a healthy body."

Next, we continue to encourage greater self-awareness. We ask you to focus on how you see yourself - your "self-image". We explore what makes you, YOU. The next chapter examines your innate talents and acknowledges the gifts you bring. We take a moment to celebrate the fabulous person you are.

[1] https://www.webmd.com/balance/stress-management/effects-of-stress-on-your-body 2017
[2] Stress in America™, 2017 survey conducted online within the United States by The Harris Poll on behalf of the American Psychological Association (APA)

REFLECTION

Review the physical symptoms mentioned, which is most likely to remind you to take better care of your needs?

How are you more aware of the triggers than you were before reading this chapter?

What surprised you the most in this chapter?

What are you willing to do differently to be healthier?

How will you share this information to gain more support?

"

When my
natural gifts
shine, I know I
am in the flow.

"

CHAPTER SEVEN
CELEBRATE YOUR INNATE GIFTS

We all deserve to be celebrated. Yet, how often do we pause to take the time to acknowledge who we really are and what we do for others? As busy individuals, we don't often appreciate our unique innate talents or notice the gifts we bring to those around us. Take this opportunity to see the real You, rediscover your worth and realize your full potential.

We are all unique. This is what makes the world so interesting, colorful and creative. There is no one else quite like you on this entire planet. Each of us have *innate gifts*. These gifts are a natural part of our demeanor and character. They are what we are born with and make us who we are at our core. Think about a baby, they are curious, funny, joyful, and so much more. YOU came into this world this way and it's still who YOU are today!

Innate gifts are a natural strength you possess that comes easily and effortlessly from the day you were born. They are not a skill you learned. For example, you may be naturally inclined to look after others, have a flair for organizing, make friends easily or quickly solve a problem. These are innate talents and are with us from day one and stay with us throughout our life. They are inborn and are the essence of who we are. Think about how your friends would describe you. Is it generous, creative, kind, strategic, or intuitive? These are your innate talents and what make up the real you.

PAUSE

On the next page circle ten innate gifts that you feel best describe who you really are. Be honest and go with your first response. There is room at the bottom of the page to write in additional gifts. Afterwards, ask a confidant, partner, or someone else you trust to name ten innate gifts (not a competency or skill, not what you've learned, rather, who you are) that best describe you and why. This gives you a wider view of how others see you and can help you embrace your unique gifts. Your innate gifts provide you with an increased awareness of who you are.

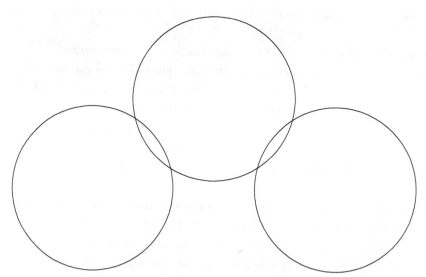

Write three of your own ideas in the circles above.

CREATIVE INSPIRING SENSITIVE

FAITHFUL LEADER FOCUSED

KIND STRATEGIC SEEKER/CURIOUS

GENEROUS CARING LOYAL

RISK-TAKER CONFIDENT COMMUNICATOR

EXPRESSIVE WISE WARM

PROBLEM SOLVER PERSUASIVE RESOURCEFUL

HUMOROUS SPIRITED HONEST

JOYFUL RESULTS DRIVEN CHARISMATIC

RESPONSIBLE INTUITIVE RESILIENT

EMPATHETIC PASSIONATE PRAGMATIC

NURTURING CALM OPTIMISTIC

VISUALLY OR RELATIONSHIP PHYSICALLY
SPATIALLY AWARE BUILDER CO-ORDINATED

COURAGEOUS ANALYTICAL FAIR

Now that you've identified your top ten gifts and have talked with those who know you best, take a moment to reflect on what you learned about yourself. Pause and recognize the uniquely, powerful individual you have always been. Given what you've learned, consider how you treat yourself.

PAUSE

Describe five ways in which you will be more caring, kind, and thoughtful to yourself. (eg: buy flowers for yourself every week, or take a long soak in a bath).

1.

2.

3.

4.

5.

Continue to play to your strengths. Be kind to yourself. Focus on what you do well and what comes easily and naturally to you rather than what you don't do well. For example, if you are a connector and naturally a relationship builder, then you might consider a job that requires those talents, or if you are a caring, nurturing individual then you might want to volunteer in the healthcare profession. Whatever your innate gifts, it's important that you feel you are using them on a regular basis whether it be in your work or in your personal life. They are a part of who you are and they need to be expressed.

You have the capacity to accept all of you, and even the bits you may find yourself criticizing. It's your time to shine. Continue to keep the negative Meddler from rearing its ugly head. And, be mindful of the joy-filled Player who encourages you to be your best self.

We have now completed Part One, of the i-Matter Equation; Self Awareness. The take-aways include a deeper understanding of your big dream, the Meddler's and Player's influence on your mental, emotional and physical wellbeing and your innate gifts. Furthermore, we have the awareness to incorporate these new learnings into our daily routine.

Part Two builds on what you've learned and delves deeper to look at how your conscious choices to date have affected self-care, your energy levels and your quality of life. You will be taking the Life Energy Inventory, an insightful and easy assessment that explores seven life areas. This tool gives you greater clarity into which areas of your life are depleted and need your attention, and which are full and thriving.

REFLECTION

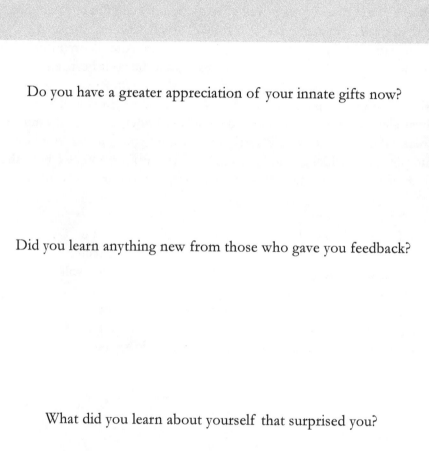

Do you have a greater appreciation of your innate gifts now?

Did you learn anything new from those who gave you feedback?

What did you learn about yourself that surprised you?

66

When you change
the way you look
at things, the
things you look at
change.

99

— **Wayne Dyer**

PART TWO
DECISION

―――――――

"The story you tell yourself
becomes self-fulfilling"

CONSCIOUS CHOICE
adj.

means being fully aware of your reality and the consequences and impact of your decision(s) before you make it, staying true to your values regardless of the internal or external pressures; recognizing your non-negotiable needs.

CHAPTER EIGHT
CONSCIOUS LIVING IS A LIFESTYLE

In Part One, we learned to be more introspective and aware of our physical, mental, and emotional barriers. We learned to recognize our internal dialogue, to focus in on the positive Player voice, to be self-reflective, and to be mindful of and grateful for the joyous moments in our daily lives. Ultimately, we want to be more aware of our stressors, energy levels and how better to manage these along our path.

Part Two focuses on the decision-making process and is the second step in the i-Matter Equation. As we've shown in Part One self-awareness is key to improving self-care. Equally important is the ability to make conscious choices that advocate well-being. Will your decisions help you to take time out to pause, follow the Player's good advice, or revert to the Meddler's poor choices? Positive decision-making leads to positive results over the days, weeks, months and years adding up to *your best life.*

We make thousands of decisions consciously or unconsciously all day, every day.

Some decisions are made under stress or when we don't have all the facts. Other decisions are made in an instant automatically, like tying your shoelaces or looking both ways before crossing the road. These instant choices are made easily and almost automatically because we are practiced and fully aware of the consequences, many of which have been learned as children or experienced often over a lifetime.

No matter how minor the decision, it is still a choice. Our chances of making better decisions requires mindful effort and an awareness of our values.

When we are faced with "big or important" choices, we typically weigh the pros and cons or discuss the impact and consequences with others before deciding. At this point, we tend to be more deliberate in our thinking.

Problems arise with the everyday decisions. These decisions may not get the same attention, often because they happen so frequently and seem less important. For example, you decide to buy something online you don't need, and still you do this every month. You go through a drive thru at a fast food place and order your favorite burger and fries on a regularly basis instead of a balanced meal at home. You go out to buy a gift and end up spending the week's budget on new makeup and perfume that you didn't really need. As a result, the consequences of these small impulsive decisions may not be weighed with the same consideration as the bigger decisions. Impulsive decision making often creates the greatest anxiety and stress over time.

It is not these one-time decisions to go "off the budget or diet" that gets us into trouble, rather it is the cumulative effect of the unconscious decisions we make on a regular basis that causes the negative impact. Interestingly, even when we choose not to decide it is still a decision. Therefore, every decision has an impact and consequence.

PAUSE

Take an honest look at the decisions you have made in the past 30 days, write down four big or small decisions. For e.g. a small decision might be going to an expensive dinner. It was fun but you are now unable to pay a bill.

DECISION	POSITIVE OR NEGATIVE IMPACT	CONSEQUENCES OR POSITIVE OUTCOMES

What did you notice about the type of decisions you are making?

We are not suggesting you create a matrix or spreadsheet every time you make a decision. However, it is important that you recognize that every choice you make or don't make has a ripple effect that can impact you, your loved ones and reach into the community. For those of you with children, consider how your choices impact them and the example you are setting.

To summarize, take notice of the decisions you are making because each one has an impact. Use your wise Player to guide you to make the best choice with all the information you gathered.

PRIORITIZING LIFE

When life's demands increase exponentially the challenge remains on how to keep the positive Player in motion. Our lives, like many of you, were packed full of competing demands and priorities. We realized we needed to find a way to pay closer attention to the quieter voice inside that was telling us to take a *deliberate pause* and *prioritize self-care*.

Once we were aware of this, we were able to create a list of what we consider "Player Priority Questions, (PPQ's)". They helped us to foster the positive Player to do what was best and right for us. We started asking each other and our friends these questions whenever we were at a crossroads or had a big decision to make.

PLAYER PRIORITY QUESTIONS (PPQ'S):

1. Will I be glad that I did it?

2. Is this a must-do or can I leave it for later?

3. Is this the best use of my time?

4. Will I feel regretful if I don't do this?

5. Will a delay cause stress?

6. Is it okay to say no to this?

7. What is stopping me?

8. What is the value of this?

These PPQ's keep the positive Player in motion by helping you to sort out what needs to be taken care of today, what can be left till tomorrow and what is no longer important. The more you apply these questions to daily life, the more they will become a natural part of your thinking and the easier it will be to prioritize and make better decisions that lead to positive change.

PAUSE

Think of a real-life situation you are currently concerned about and ask yourself one or two PPQ questions to help you clarify your thoughts.

You are at a crossroads:

- A friend wants you to do something and you don't.

- You have an important decision that needs to be made in twenty-four hours.

- You have an unexpected problem or dilemma.

- You are thinking of making a big change in your life (job, relationship).

- You want to make quality time for yourself.

Your question:

Your answer:

What did you discover when you asked yourself the PPQ questions?

These key PPQ's help determine whether something is a real priority or not. We use these PPQ's with our friends, clients and of course with each other. They have kept us on our path and prevented us from wasting valuable time. We encourage you to ask yourself or a trusted friend the questions to stay focused on what matters most to you.

They will help you to make choices that are in your best interest and lead you to living a more enjoyable life.

Use this opportunity to forgive past regrets, be kind and recognize the future lies in the conscious choices you make going forward.

As we move through our lives at full speed, we often forget to pause. In doing so, the consequences of our hasty decisions can create further problems, conflicts and challenges. These impulsive, unhealthy choices eventually catch up with us and have a profound impact on our relationships, and our well-being. The reality is every choice big or small has an impact on our life for better or worse.

We know from our own personal experiences that a stressful, hurried pace of life can get in the way of making the right and best decisions for us. Michael Mauboussin [1], a Columbia Business School professor says, "Fight-or-flight mode is good for some things, but decision-making is not among them -- especially for important, long-term decisions."

As a result, stress can hinder good decision making creating greater problems down the road like a lack of self-care. It is important to recognize this fact and to be aware of the decisions that increase stress. Being conscious of the choices you make takes practice. It has been shown that to change a habit or cultivate a new behavior requires making small incremental movements daily and over time, rather than pressuring ourselves to do it all at once.

PRACTICE PRIORITIZING

For the next twenty-one days, practice a 15
minute pause each morning. Reflect on what your
top three priorities are for that day.[2]

The twenty-one days cultivates positive habits by giving the
process time to unfold, and the commitment you make to
deepen over time. This enables the changes you make to stick.
What's surprising is how few people practice this in their
daily lives. The truth is that we go about our daily lives
just doing what we always do because that's what we're
used to doing. And, it's easier that way, even if our lives
are not what we truly want - a more joy-filled life.

We have learned over the past several chapters how to be more
aware of our thoughts, and what drives our decisions. Living
a conscious lifestyle requires practice, willpower and regular
reflection. Stay alert to the Meddler , your inner critic, who
sabotages you to make unconscious choices that don't benefit
you. Tune in instead to the Player who encourages you to
stop and take a pause to do what is right and best for you.

The next chapter looks at where your energy is depleted
and what areas need energizing. We are now well on
our way to gathering the tools in our toolbox that
support us in living a conscious and joy-filled life.

[1] Michael Mauboussin, Think Twice: Harnessing the Power of Counterintuition, 2009
[2] NLP https://en.wikipedia.org/wiki Neuro-linguistic_programming)

REFLECTION

How can you be more aware of the conscious choices you make?

After reading this chapter, what new action will you take?

What was the greatest learning for you in this chapter?

"

The choices you make influence the quality of your day-to-day life.

"

CHAPTER NINE
THE LIFE ENERGY INVENTORY™

The best decisions are the ones aligned with our priorities and values. Let's dig a little deeper to discover whether you are living your best life based on your values. In this chapter, you will have the opportunity to take The Life Energy Inventory™ (LEI). It's a practical and easy assessment tool that targets seven key areas of your life. We consider this a whole life review that focuses on the following seven areas: mind, body, soul, heart, philanthropy, creativity and career/financial.

The purpose is to determine which of these areas, despite being a priority, may have been neglected due to stress, a lack of willpower or busyness. The LEI determines where your energy levels are at present, which areas are thriving, and which need more attention.

According to a Gallup study on Wellbeing and the Five Essential Elements [1], research scientists, psychologists, and economists with over fifty years of collected works agree that there are five universal elements of well-being that differentiate a thriving life from one spent suffering.

The five broad categories essential to most people are career, liking what you do every day; social, having love and strong relationships; financial, managing your economic life; physical, having good health and enough energy; and community, giving back to foster a sense of engagement. These essential elements need to be nurtured regularly to achieve maximum well-being.

Maintaining this balancing act is often challenging even for those of us who have self-awareness. Use this assessment tool to take a personal inventory of where your energy levels are currently depleted and make conscious choices that propel you forward.

When we don't value ourselves enough to put us on our own to do list, or find time to prioritize our needs alongside our other demands, then stress levels invariably increase and wellbeing decreases. You are accountable for the choices you make and, therefore, how your life is showing up.

According to the American Psychological Association's (APA's) report, "Stress in America™: The State of Our Nation" 2017. [2].

- Almost one-third (31%) of employed adults have difficulty managing

- Over one third (35%) cite jobs interfering with their family or personal

- Stress causes more than half of Americans (54%) to fight with people

- One in four people report that they have been alienated from a friend or family member because of stress

The statistics show many of us struggle to find a happy middle ground. When our energy levels are depleted in one area, it has a ripple effect on other areas. For example, if you decide to spend more time at work, your own health and personal relationships may suffer; or if your relationships is your only focus, you might be neglecting your body or creative side. Realistically, you can't have every area in life at 100% all the time. However, if you have a heightened awareness then you can manage your life better. The assessment helps you hone in on what areas are depleted and what areas are full. It's a personal choice about where and how you want to spend your time.

"

For there is
nothing either
good or bad - but
thinking makes it
so.

— Shakespeare

ASSESSMENT

Be honest and answer with your first response.
This is not about trying to get a perfect score rather an accurate picture of where you are today. It takes about 20-25 minutes of focused time to complete. Or if you prefer to take the assessment online, visit www.energycatalystgroup.com/Services/whatwedo or www.15minutepause.com.

Using the scale from 1-10
(1 = strongly disagree and 10 = strongly agree),
rate each statement based on how you are currently living your life.

Ignore the letters on the left for now, they will help you with scoring later.

LIFE ENERGY INVENTORY™

1 = *Strongly Disagree*
3 = *Disagree Somewhat*
5 = *Agree Somewhat*
10 = *Strongly Agree*

_____ **A**   I have goals and I achieve them

_____ **B**   I enjoy the value of spending time by myself

_____ **C**   I do as much as I can for the worthy causes I believe in

_____ **D**   I have a creative side and ideas, which I develop and express regularly

_____ **E**   It's easy for me to quiet my mind

_____ **F**   I make the time to eat well-balanced meals daily

_____ **G**   I prioritize quality time with my loved ones regularly

_____ **A**   When I have innovative work ideas, I champion them

_____ **B**   I am resilient and able to deal with life's difficulties

_____ **C**   I make time to ensure that I have a legacy to leave behind

_____ **D**   I find time to spend on fun activities that I enjoy like cooking, gardening

_____ **E**   I keep my mind stimulated and rarely feel bored

_____ **F**   I am fit and healthy

_____ **G**   I leave work on time regularly to spend time with people who matter most to me

_____ **A**   I am energized by the tasks I do daily at work

_____ **B**   I know what my life purpose is and am fulfilling it

_____ **C**   I like to volunteer and find the time to do so

_____ **D**   I put time aside regularly to concentrate on my interests and crafts (e.g.. artistic or home improvement)

_____ **E**   I regularly sleep well through the night because my mind is calm

_____ **F**   I am happy with the way my body looks

_____ **G**   When I take vacations, I leave work behind so I can relax with loved ones (family, kids, friends)

_____ **A**   I am content with my career path (e.g. homemaker, entrepreneur, employee)

_____ **B**   I have a daily practice of prayer meditation, time alone that fosters my religious, spiritual pursuits or sense of peace

_____ **C**   I find ways to help my community on a regular basis

_____ **D**   I am aware of how to stimulate my creative side

_____ **E**   I turn off my technological gadgets in order to give my mind a rest everyday

_____ **F**   I take time out to regularly pamper myself (i.e., massage)

_____ **G**   I resolve conflicts easily with the people that matter to me

_____ **A**   I save or invest regularly based on my household income

_____ **B**   I have a daily practice of being in gratitude

_____ **C**   I give money regularly to the causes that matter to me

_____ **D**   I have joined a group and am doing the thing I love (e.g. dancing, playing an instrument)

_____ **E**   I am mentally able to juggle everything without dropping anything on my plate

_____ **F**   I am appreciated and loved by the people around me

_____ **G**   I don't suffer regularly from aches and pains

_____ **A**   I am fulfilling my career potential

_____ **B**   I am able to forgive and forget so past baggage does not influence my present

_____ **C**   I donate my time or money to my past college, my children's school, or other areas that have meaning for me

_____ **D**   I feel at ease contributing ideas and giving my opinion as I think they are of value

_____ **E**   My negative mind chatter does not dominate my thinking on a daily basis

_____ **F**   I am content with my sex life

_____ **G**   I devote one on one time to my kids, partner or friends

_____ **A**   I am okay with the amount of total debt I currently have (credit cards and loans)

_____ **B**   I feel my life is fulfilled at a deep level

_____ **C**   I sign up for volunteer expeditions with Volunteer Service Organizations

_____ **D**   I am playful and curious

_____ **E**   I am able to overcome my negative mind chatter with positive affirmations

_____ **F**   I rarely get sick

_____ **G**   I am happy with my relationship status i.e. single, married, or divorced

_____ **A**   I am content with my financial earnings and status

_____ **B**   I have a strong faith that I am on my right life path

_____ **C**   I find ways on a daily basis to give back (put money in someone else's meter or give food to a homeless person)

_____ **D**   I am spontaneous and spend time on the activities I enjoy irrespective of life's many ups and downs

_____ **E**   I am able to deal with emerging problems easily

_____ **F**   I take care of my body even when I am stressed

_____ **G**   I have people in my life who make me laugh and smile often

_____ **A**   I like my work environment

_____ **B**   I live my life in the present

_____ **C**   I regularly budget for my philanthropic causes

_____ **D**   I carve out time regularly to do the things I really enjoy

_____ **E**   I face my fears and do it anyway

_____ **F**   I exercise 3-4 times a week

_____ **G**   I listen to my heart and follow my feelings regularly

_____ **A**   I am proactive about my career developments

_____ **B**   I live my life with integrity

_____ **C**   I donate time to my favorite causes

_____ **D**   I make time to enjoy the arty, creative sides of my personality like music, astronomy, going to museums or galleries

_____ **E**   I rarely regret the decisions I make

_____ **F**   I eat plenty of vegetables and fruit every day

_____ **G**   I forgive and don't hold grudges

POINTS SCORED

- Each question has a letter next to it (A, B, C, D, E, F, or G).
- Add up the totals for each of the letters A, B, C, D, E, F or G.
- Put your score for each category next to the corresponding letter in the totals box on the opposite page
- This is your percentage for that area.

   A - *Career / Financial*

   B - *Soul*

   C - *Philanthropy*

   D - *Creativity*

   E - *Mind*

   F - *Body*

   G - *Heart*

CATEGORY	SCORE
A	
B	
C	
D	
E	
F	
G	

Below are diagrams of your
LIFE ENERGY TANKS.

Color them in to represent your scores.

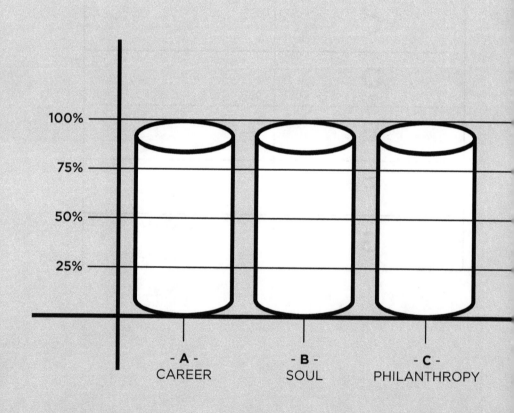

For example, if A (Career/Financial), equals 50 percent then color in your tank to 50 percent on the tank labeled Career. If B (Soul) equals 15 percent, then similarly color it in on the tank labeled Soul at 15 percent. Review all the colored in tanks to get an idea of what your life energy balance looks like.

The lower your score, the more depleted your life energy tank and the higher the score, the more energized you are in that area.

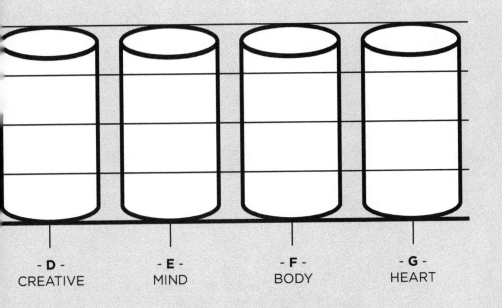

- **D** -
CREATIVE

- **E** -
MIND

- **F** -
BODY

- **G** -
HEART

For a detailed explanation of what your results mean, go to the Appendix and read pages 181-191. The scores are divided into three groups 0-50 percent, 51-74 percent and 75-100 percent. If your energy tanks are below 50 percent, consider this area depleted and in need of urgent care. If your score is between 51-74 percent, this area needs some attention and it's up to you to decide how much time and energy you spend improving it. If your score is above 75 percent, then your energy tank is full, yet requires regular maintenance.

PAUSE

After having completed the LEI, review your scores to see which areas are depleted and where you need to focus more of your attention.

Is it your mind, body, creativity or one of the other categories?

Write down your top two highest scores and lowest scores below:

Highest:
        1.

        2.

Lowest:
        1.

        2.

Consider your scores a snapshot of where you are today.
At any time, these scores can shift based on your life
circumstances, or changes you've made. We recommend taking
it in three to six months' time to see what has changed.

This information provides valuable insights of how well you prioritize
your life based on your values and needs. If you're disappointed
that your scores are not as high as expected, you are not alone. The
majority of those who have taken the assessment including some of
Michelle's clients, had scores below 50% in more than one area.

The LEI results have shown you how you're leading your life
presently. Now it's up to you to decide what you are going to
do about it. Are you going to make real change or continue on
autopilot doing what you've always done? Be aware of the negative
Meddler whose voice might get louder and try to keep you stuck.

Did you know that 70 percent of adults [1] have been recommended
by a healthcare provider to make lifestyle and behavior changes? Yet,
according to the American Psychological Association, **"Many are
too stressed to manage their stress to make these changes."**

And, the barriers reported to making lifestyle changes include:
- Lack of willpower (33 percent),
- Too much stress (20 percent),
- Lack of confidence (14 percent) [2]

We understand it's difficult to make change. These statistics are
an indication of how a negative mindset and stress can make it
even more challenging to do something positive for ourselves.

What actions are you willing to take now to improve your
lowest scores? We have over hundred suggestions in Part Three.
Go to the chapter area where you're lowest and pick one or
two actions to begin replenishing or make up your own.

LOW SCORE ACTION PLAN

1.

2.

The truth is that we all have life areas that are more depleted than others. The good news is now you have an increased awareness and because of that can make conscious choices to do something different to recharge and refill those areas. This is your reminder to make choices that benefit you, no matter what else is going on.

Part Three focuses on refilling your energy tanks to reduce stress and feel more energized. It's up to you to put yourself first because you matter. Take the opportunity and spend your 15 minutes of 'me time' on an area that is depleted. The last part of this playbook is divided into seven life areas that can be dipped into and out of depending on your mood and need.

[1]Gallup, on Well-being, the Five Essential Elements,
by Tom Rath & Jim Harter, May 2012
[2]Stress in America, American Psychological Association, 2017
http://www.apa.org/news/press/releases/2017/11/lowest-point.aspx

REFLECTION

What did you learn about your energy levels and energy tanks?

Were you surprised by the results? If so, why or why not?

Given what you learned, what will you do differently?

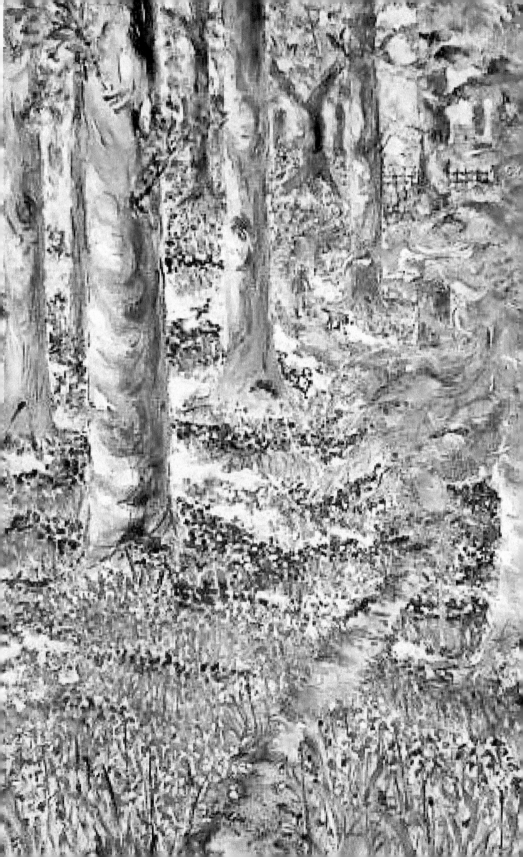

PURPOSEFUL ACTION

"The busier you are,
the more self-care you need."

"

Make a
choice to
enjoy your
life!

"

CHAPTER TEN
ENERGY BOOST

The third and final phase of the playbook integrates all that you've learned so far. We've guided you to spend time being self-reflective and to make conscious decisions that benefit you. Now it's time to take purposeful action. This is the last step in the i-Matter Equation. The next few chapters include a multitude of imaginative and heartfelt ideas that can be incorporated into your busy day in just 15 minutes. Easy and doable given that time is a premium in all our lives.

This pause will give you time to unplug and recharge — we call this your *recovery time*. Olympians, top athletes and performers all do this and it is what makes them excellent. They understand they can push themselves to a point and then they need time to recover. The same is true for us in the way we live our lives. We can go at full speed; however, we need to build in time to *pause and recover*, to find the space to relax our mind, our body, our heart so we are re-energized to engage back at work, with our kids, partner, and community.

Energy is the ultimate currency. Energy to be present in your life, to engage fully with each human being you touch, with your senses, your body, your work and your family. Having energy to connect to what is important creates joy and fulfillment [1].

At the end of Part Two, you've identified your top two highest and lowest scores. Part Three is dedicated to help you refill your lowest tanks. We provide 175 self-care suggestions that can enrich your mind, body, career, fulfill your heart's desire, uncover your soul purpose, embrace your philanthropic side, and access your creativity.

This part is designed to be flexible. You can read it from start to finish or skip to the chapter that has significant meaning to you based on your Life Energy Inventory™ scores. The following chapters inspire you to take thoughtful action to make long-lasting change in short, doable 15 minute increments.

Some of the ideas may take less than 15 minutes, and others can be achieved over the long term in 15 minute increments. The ideas are thoughtful, fun, silly, and sometimes thought-provoking or challenging. For example, you might choose to sit in silence, learn a musical instrument, put your phone away while at dinner, write a love letter, or build a hobby into a business. Taking a small doable 15 minute pause regularly, provides big rewards; as a result, a burden may be lifted, a promise implemented, or a sense of achievement felt.

If you have a larger goal or project you want to tackle, breaking it down into bite sized chunks is much easier. Many of us assume it takes an hour to do anything, think again. 15 minutes of 'me time' is doable. As we mentioned in the beginning of the book, carving out 15 minutes everyday adds up to almost two hours a week, almost eight hours a month and about 91 hours per year. Our own personal experiences show that this is enough time to reflect, start a project, change a habit and reduce stress. This is a long-term commitment and depends on you being consistent. Start taking 15 minute walks every day at lunch time or at the end of the day, or make a healthy meal or snack, and bring it to work. To help you stay motivated, ask a partner or friend to join you or encourage you.

There might be times when you feel too tired to take time for yourself and that is okay. Understand this is not another "thing" to add to your to-do list. Rather, it's about re-prioritizing and making a conscious choice to be joy-filled and kinder to yourself. Author, Jan Hanson, MS, LAc, co-author of Mother Nurture: A

Mother's Guide to Health in Body, Mind, and Intimate Relationships [2], said, "It's a plain fact: You have to keep refilling your own cup in order to pour into your kids [or job]—let alone have anything left over for your husband [or wife] or yourself."

From our experience, we know that there will be days when you just won't feel like it. We all have days when we fall back into familiar patterns or get off track. That is not the time to beat yourself up or hold onto your guilt, because then you'll be letting the negative Meddler, the sabotager, get the better of you. Keep reminding yourself that this is your time, and you deserve some joy in your life.

Part Three is your opportunity to take purposeful action in the form of a daily 15 minute ritual. It means putting yourself on your agenda. This 15 minute pause helps you to recharge and reignite joy before you are overly stressed, exhausted and unable to care for others. Whatever area you choose to energize, let it satisfy your needs, relieve your stress levels, and revitalize your life.

[1] Mark Hyman, MD, The Third Metric: The Two Steps to Solving Our Real Energy Crisis from Huffington Post

[2 Jan Hanson, MS, LAc, co-author of Mother Nurture: A Mother's Guide to Health in Body, Mind, and Intimate Relationships

" It's not just a job; make it meaningful. **"**

CHAPTER ELEVEN
CAREER & FINANCIAL ASPIRATIONS

Did you know that we spend more time working than we do anything else, including sleeping? Since this is our reality, do you enjoy what you do for a living? If not, why not? This chapter focuses on how to find fulfillment in our job and the reality of balancing this while ensuring we meet our financial obligations.

There are challenges to doing what we love while still paying the bills. Maybe we want to follow a passion, own a business, be an entrepreneur, be a stay at home mother, move up the corporate ladder, add skills to our current job, get a promotion, or go back to school to pursue a hobby or new career. Whatever it is you desire, the first steps are to reassess where you are presently, identify what motivates you and make changes to meet your wants. Are you looking for job security, an increase in salary, good working relationships, an energizing work environment, acknowledgment, or hoping to be a part of something that is greater than you are?

If you are unsatisfied, get creative about how to make a change. This may require thinking outside the box and expanding your options.

The truth is most people view work as a means to an end. Defining what a career means to us is critical if we want to find true fulfillment. A career is not just a nine to five job, rather a lifestyle. It allows us to take pride in what we do and do our best at it. Being our best self in whatever we choose to do brings great satisfaction.

When Michelle started her consulting and coaching practice many years ago, she knew she had to get a part-time job. She worked at a retail store to ensure she could pay her bills while building her client base. As her business grew over the first year, Michelle was able to cut back her hours and eventually quit her part-time job. Knowing what she wanted and willing to do what was needed created the career she dreamed of. It meant doing things in a different way, yet the risk was worth it. Her consulting practice is thriving today.

MANIFEST

Choose one of the ideas below to fulfill your career or financial aspirations:

1. Look for ways to improve your present job environment (make a list, present it to your manager).

2. Research careers in an industry you have an interest in.

3. With a colleague or your team, brainstorm a solution that has been bothering you.

4. Make plans to meet with a different colleague or business associate each week or month to build a professional network of relationships.

5. Write freely for 15 minutes about where you would like to be in your career in six months, and one year (no censoring).

6. Update your résumé or bio, and ask a trusted friend for feedback.

7. Mentor someone who needs help in his or her career or job.

8. Read about the latest trends in the career you have or want.

9. Set up a regular savings account and have an automatic amount put in it every month.

10. Find a coach and set up a 15-minute weekly or monthly call.

11. Research conferences that you could attend to learn and network.

12. Create an *Acknowledgment* box, file or folder, add compliments, praises or acknowledgments into it and refer to it when you need a reminder of what a great job you are doing.

13. Ask a friend that has a different perspective to brainstorm new career ideas (no limitations just throw ideas out).

14. Call your credit card company and ask to lower your interest rate or cut up or close one or two credit cards with the highest interest rate.

15. Make your workplace appealing and personal to you. Bring flowers, hang a photo or picture you love on the wall in your workspace.

16. Write down the top five values that are important to you in a career or workplace and see if it matches the place you currently work.

17. Honestly assess your work-style, what you really want (a part-time job, a job you share, a schedule that allows you to leave at three) and discuss with your boss to see how you can create this.

18. Make an appointment with a career counselor or coach if you are in transition or returning to work after a long absence.

19. If you have a business idea, research it, do a SWOT (strengths, weaknesses, opportunities, threats) and cost analysis, look at competitors, find your unique selling point - start building it up in small 15 minute increments.

20. Identify a skill to learn or improve and sign up for a webinar or class.

21. Set up a direct debit to make a payment to your credit cards.

22. Schedule a monthly 15 minute meeting with your manager to ask for feedback so you know how you are really doing and what can be improved upon.

23. Trade services and skills with a friend - learn what they do, and in return, they can learn what you do.

24. Set specific and measurable goals for yourself with a deadline and ask a friend or co-worker to help you stay on track.

25. Put a list of accomplishments (e.g., saving costs, new process,) together and speak to your manager about taking on a new responsibility or ask what you need to do to get a promotion. Be proactive.

REFLECTION

What have you changed to fulfill your career aspirations? Be specific.

What are you doing differently to take care of your financial needs?

"

When we are
content with
who we are,
the rest will
follow.

"

CHAPTER TWELVE
SOUL PURPOSE

Those who have a healthy connection to the soul on a deeper
level know the value of unconditional love of self. There are
many ways to connect to the soul e.g. love, higher power, spirit,
inner voice, God, Allah, Buddah, Muhommad and others. When
we feed our soul, the negative influences from the outside world
have less power over us. This simply means that no matter what
chaos or uncertainty is going on around us, we are able to regain
a sense of calm and get back to a centered place at our core.
Happiness on the inside equates to happiness on the outside.

Are you dealing with problems that seem to be out of your control?
Is the negative meddler or other drainers getting the best of you?
If you find yourself internally conflicted, possibly obsessing over
your failures, or upset about how life has gone so far, then you will
benefit by nurturing your soul. Soul purpose is the Player voice that
believes—despite all the naysayers and negative circumstances—that
good will prevail. It's the tiny voice that says you are loved, valued and
accepted for being you. When we listen more intently to the Player
voice, we are encouraged to engage in greater self-love and care.
A positive outlook encourages us to be more forgiving and kinder
towards ourselves and those around us. Being soul-filled allows us to
come from a place of love rather than fear, anxiety, doubt or anger.

Live in the now. Be fully present.
Be attentive to what you are doing, feeling, seeing, and thinking.

PAUSE

Put your bare feet firmly on the ground and feel your feet touching the ground and notice the way it feels; is the ground hard, cushioned, hot, cold and how do your feet actually feel? Is it comforting knowing your feet are on solid ground?

Jane, a single forty-year-old, found she was spending considerably more time at work than anywhere else, living on take-out and running on empty. She had felt a longing inside her yet, she couldn't find the breathing space to pause and consider what this feeling meant. Exhausted, she had no option but to take time away from all of life's demands. She planned a meditative holiday. During this time she slept more, ate well and had a chance to reflect and recuperate. She realized she needed more time with loved ones and that she was ready to find love and be loved. As a result she decided to look for love online. One night she wrote down what she wanted in a mate, and what was important to her in a relationship. Each evening for fifteen minutes, she made a concerted effort to stay open to the potential partners she met. Imagine her surprise when after several dates, she met a man whom she knew was her "Mr. Right." A year later, she was married.

How much of you do you give to others? Isn't it equally important to give back to yourself? The way we treat ourselves, impacts and influences all our other relationships. When we take care of ourselves the more energy we have to give back to others. We all need time to recharge if we want to handle life's various up and downs in a healthy way.

When we pause to feed our souls we gain greater strength and energy to deal with our fears and resentments that may keep us stuck. Finding time to be alone is also beneficial as it allows for self-reflection. Being alone and lonely are not the same. In fact, feeding the soul fills the empty space inside that is commonly called loneliness.

Take time to re-engage with your authentic self at your core. This is your internal powerhouse and the essence of who you are. When you nurture it, you bring peace and satisfaction to your life. Those who are soul-filled radiate positivity and a sense of well-being. Feed your soul to bolster inner strength, increase self-worth, self-respect and self-love.

RADIATE

Choose one or more of the following ideas to nurture your soul.

1. Make peace with your past so it won't interfere with your future—write a letter to yourself.

2. Create your own mantra, paste it on your bathroom wall, and repeat it 10 or more times (for example, "I deserve the best that life has to offer"). Say it till you believe it.

3. Apologize to someone and really mean it.

4. Write an email, card or note to thank a friend for the difference he or she has made in your life.

5. Find a place you love. Sit still and truly be present. What do you see and hear?

6. Write down the secret wishes or desires that you want to see happen in the next month, 6 months or year.

7. Make a dream board and add to it. Use pictures and words to depict all that your soul wants to attract.

8. Sit, relax, and close your eyes. Realize how much you are loved for all that you do and for all that you are.

9. Forgive yourself or someone else, and if needed let this person know that you forgive them.

10. Journal without stopping or correcting yourself every morning before you start the day. A great way to connect to your inner self.

11. Visit Brad Yates's website, http://www.bradyates.net/youtube.html.

12. Call a friend and have a fifteen-minute "pity party" about something that you are "stuck" in. Then release it and commit not to bring it up again.

13. Before going to sleep, pause for a gratitude moment: name three reasons for being grateful.

14. Let go of a grudge you've been holding, and tell the person in person, by phone or in writing. Anger breeds more anger, which leads to poor health.

15. Review and reflect on all of your innate talents and revisit them when you are having a bad day.

16. Divide a piece of paper into three, write down your list of worries in one column, your feelings in the next and in the third, write an action you will take to let it go or burn the paper and release the worries.

17. Pray in whatever form that takes for you.

18. Be present for a full fifteen minutes. Whatever you are doing or whomever you are with, be fully present. Don't let your thoughts distract you or outside noises like your phone get in the way.

19. When in an argument, take fifteen minutes to reframe your feelings and put yourself in the other person's shoes before re-engaging.

20. Write down a list of what you have loved,
    learned, and achieved, and how you've grown.
    Acknowledge how far you've come!

21. Plan a weekend retreat for yourself or with your
    best friend, book it online and commit to going.

22. Imagine you had a month to live, write down
    everything you'd want to do. Choose one and
    start doing it and continue the list.

23. Make a collage of inspiring quotes that motivate
    you. Hang this on your fridge or mirror.

24. Find a quiet, peaceful place you consider your sanctuary,
    a place of worship, a mosque, temple, church or
    ocean and listen to what your soul has to say.

25. Explore the concept of the soul in
    books, podcasts or audio CD's.

REFLECTION

Take a moment and pause. What does your soul need?

Find an affirmation that resonates and say it out loud when you

are feeling lost or stuck.

You are My Friends and Family

If you have desires, memories,
wants and needs,
Then, you definitely are my
friends and family.
For, I too have desires, memories, wants
and needs.

If you have doubts or become confused
in life, even once,
If you have goals, dreams and a
wondering mind,
If you seek love, joy and happiness,
Then you are my friends and family.

Manijeh Motaghy
Mindfulness Teacher
an excerpt from Manijeh

"

The seeds you
plant today
will define the
legacy you leave
tomorrow.

"

CHAPTER THIRTEEN
THE GIFT OF GIVING

Are you giving to give back or are you giving to get something back? That is the difference between someone who is philanthropic and someone who is self-serving. The purpose of being philanthropic is to make a difference in the lives around you *without expecting anything in return*. When you help someone else, you help yourself. Doing "good" for others makes you feel good about yourself, even for 15 minutes. If you are depleted in this area consider this a time to do something for someone else—with no expectations and thereby, you won't feel resentful.

Being philanthropic takes on many forms; it isn't just about sending money for a cause you believe in (although that is certainly one way). When you spend fifteen minutes truly being thoughtful and genuine in your actions and words, a lasting memory is created. Your philanthropic effort must have real meaning, whether you are giving back to your family, friends, neighborhood, local school, religious or spiritual organization, the larger community, or a charitable cause. Think about it: when you give unconditionally to others, it touches the lives of those around you, and it makes you feel good, too.

Maureen is an executive assistant for a prestigious company. She works full time and has a husband and two children. She was doing as much as she could and felt something was missing. On a trip to Eastern Europe, Maureen was taken to an orphanage. There she was moved by the children and by the lack of books, *toys, and facilities. On returning home, she was compelled to do something. It started simply with a rummage through her cupboard. She started decluttering and found old books and toys to send to the orphanage. Then she wrote an e-mail to her colleagues that took less than ten minutes to write, followed by an advertisement in the local supermarket. To date, she has raised more than $100,000 dollars and continues to build on that simple start.*

There are many ways of giving. Michelle regularly pays the toll fee for the person in the car behind her when driving over a bridge or toll road. She enjoys seeing the look of surprise and knowing she has made someone's day. This idea started over twenty years ago. At the time, she was crossing the Golden Gate Bridge and didn't have enough money to pay the toll. She had to pull over, go in, and write a check for two dollars. She didn't want anyone else to experience the humiliation that she felt at the time.

Similarly, one of her friends puts extra quarters in parking meters when she leaves or when she notices they are about to expire. It is a small cost to pay and yet, the rewards are great because it makes her day and no doubt that of someone else's.

PAY IT FORWARD

Decide on one or more of the following ideas and start today to give back to those who need it most.

1. Call a friend who is struggling and offer support.

2. When you see someone in need when you are out shopping, ask if you can help.

3. Make someone's day, spend a moment and thoughtfully acknowledge the service you are receiving from the grocery clerk, butcher, hairdresser, or gardener (give a genuine compliment).

4. Paint or create something and donate
   it to a charity for auction.

5. Donate blood at your local blood bank.

6. Help a neighbor in need like an elderly person
   who may need their garden weeded, pick up a
   prescription or drive them to an appointment.

7. Pick up groceries for someone who is
   sick while you do your shopping.

8. Make an appointment to visit an assisted living home or a
   children's unit and make someone's day (e.g. bring flowers).

9. Make a plate of brownies or a basket of fruit and
   take it to work the next day, or your kid's class.

10. Put five or ten cents a day in a jar (have kids participate
    if it's age appropriate) and give it all at year end to
    a good cause. Inspire others to do the same.

11. Recycle or pick up garbage in your neighborhood.

12. De-clutter in small steps e.g. your wardrobe,
    house and give what you no longer want, does
    not fit or are out of style to charity.

13. Find a coin, pick it up and pass it on to someone else.

14. Treat a friend to something special that
    they would not do for themselves.

15. Give your leftovers or buy food for a homeless person.

16. Sort through your canned goods, and take
    a bag to your local food bank.

17. Go through old books or children's books,
and donate them to your local library.

18. Make chicken soup and take it to a sick friend or coworker.

19. Find out where you can volunteer locally
and use your skills to help them.

20. Apply for a charitable bike, run or walk, ask a friend
to join you and raise money for that cause.

21. Join a group that helps kids to improve reading. Research
schools or libraries that ask for this or donate books
and send out an email to friends to do the same.

22. Organize a neighborhood garage sale with friends
and send the proceeds to a charity of choice.

23. Computers are of great value in schools in poorer
countries where they cannot afford them. Bring
your old computers to a charity that needs them.
Ask your neighbors if they want to donate.

24. Clear out your closet or choose clothes you have
not worn in a long time and give to a friend
or someone else who could use them.

25. Bake cookies and have a bake sale, donate the
money to a cause or your neighborhood school.

REFLECTION

Have you helped someone with no expectations of getting something back in return? If so, how did it feel? If not, why not?

What will you do today to make a difference in someone else's life?

Who can you help that really needs it? Name them here and then commit to do it.

"

Follow your
passion and you
will never stray
far from your
life path.

"

CHAPTER FOURTEEN
CREATIVE CATALYST

Creativity is about having fun and being curious about the world. It means opening ourselves up to new possibilities and expressing ourselves in a different way. As we nurture new ideas and try new things, we stimulate our imaginations. This might mean re-igniting a passion that we enjoyed when we were younger. Think back to your childhood; what were your hobbies or what games did you play? This is the time to listen to the Player, take a risk, do something new, or fulfill a lifelong passion.

The point is to get outside our comfort zone; unleash our courageous playful spirit, throw caution out the window, and do something new irrespective of whether we are good at it or not. Think back to the Dream Big section in Chapter Two. What did you wish for or want to pursue? If you are unsure about how to feed your creativity, watch children play. Notice how they make things up. Children are innately creative. They don't have the same limitations adults do, and this explains why they create freely and don't get bogged down by too many worries and concerns. Practice engaging your positive Player and ignore the negative Meddler.

Most great entrepreneurs, artists, and musicians have learned the art of feeding their creativity by listening to their internal player, their gut instinct or intuition. By taking the opportunity to pause one creative step at a time, we can begin to nurture our innate talents and unleash the joy that lies within all of us.

Paul is a dad with two girls under ten. He works full-time as a consultant. He commutes to work daily, which takes an hour one-way. He has a lot of day-to-day responsibilities, not including spending time with his family, his chores, and his work commitments. Paul noticed he was becoming more irritable and difficult to live with. One day he went into the attic and saw a guitar he'd bought himself many years earlier; he had never found the time to learn to play it. He brought it down and started strumming it for ten to fifteen minutes every now and then. What he found was a new passion, something that defined who he was away from everything else in his life. Today he is part of a band with a group of guys in the neighborhood. They have played to audiences, and who knows where they will go from there.

PLAY TIME

Choose one or more of the following ideas
to ignite your creative potential.

1. Go to a park and find a swing set. Swing as high
    as you can go, just like when you were a child.

2. Pot a plant or start an herb or vegetable garden.

3. Paint, draw, or color. It doesn't matter if
    you are good or not—just do it.

4. Read an inspiring page or two by the author
    SARK and explore your creative self.

5. Journal or write the first pages of a book.

6. Step into an art gallery, photography gallery, or exhibition.

7. Learn something new and discover your passion
    e.g., a language, musical instrument or karate.

8. Have game night with family or friends - play charades.

9. Make rice crispy treats or some other childhood favorite goodies for yourself or your kids.

10. Create something out of clay.

11. Explore a new part of town you have not been to before.

12. Grab your camera/phone and take some fun photos of your neighborhood, family or somewhere that you love.

13. Make a birthday, thank-you, or congratulations card rather than buying one.

14. Wear a different color outfit than you typically do, and go with what your mood reflects.

15. Redecorate by changing the furniture around in one of your rooms.

16. Create a fun family short video.

17. Write a list of fun things you've always wanted to do, choose one and check it off until you've done all of them.

18. Go through old family photos and put them in an album or in frames.

19. Start a DIY (do it yourself) home improvement project or complete one.

20. Clean your garage or basement. Assign everyone a section and give a prize to the one who does the best. It will be done in no time.

21. Ask a few friends to exchange their favorite recipes with you or try one of those quick and easy recipes that take less than 15 minutes.

22. Write a few lyrics to a song if you have a melody in you.

23. Be curious and try a new route to work,
    or new holiday destination.

24. Create birthday or party theme gifts: find a jar,
    decorate it and put in cookie dough, jam or
    popcorn. Make candles, soap or facial scrubs.

25. Host a scavenger hunt in your neighborhood
    with friends, family or children.

REFLECTION

What did you do today to refill your creative cup?

How has expressing your creative side shifted your mindset?

Have you noticed a ripple effect in any other aspect of your life?
How does it feel?

"

Calm your mind, cultivate silence.

"

CHAPTER FIFTEEN
MINDFUL MATTERS

The mind is a powerful asset and like any other organ, it needs equal rest and stimulation. Think of this chapter in two ways: For those of you with an overactive mind, consider this is an opportunity to quiet the mind, and calm the senses. For those of you who want to activate the mind, consider this a mental workout.

CALMING THE MIND

As we learned in chapters three and four, as well as in the life energy inventory, the negative Meddler has greater control over our thoughts and mind when we are depleted. When our minds are hyperactive and overstimulated, exhausted or occupied by a running "to-do list", recognize this as a sign to still the mind. Recent studies at Duke Medical School show that silence influences the development of new cells associated with learning and memory [1]. Billionaire Ray Dalio credits 'Transcendental Meditation' as the single biggest influence of his life [2].

When we give our brain a rest like we do our bodies, we gain lots of benefits, whether it's meditation or paying attention to the Player voice inside. The Player reminds us to breathe, to reflect, and to rest our mind from all the chatter inside our head. If you want to quiet the mind, then choose an appropriate option below.

If you don't use it, you will lose it. So, keep your mind fit and active.

If you want to improve your mind power, your mental outlook or your memory, review the options below. Whether you want to inspire your imaginative and creative right brain or use your logical and analytical left brain, have fun. These ideas will help you to stay positive, encourage you to be proactive, and empower your inner Player to minimize the destructive Meddler. By keeping your mind alert and agile, you have the capacity to grow, learn, and expand your thinking.

Chris, who is in her sixties, was worried that she wasn't doing enough to keep her mind active. She bought a Sudoku book and began doing the easy puzzles first. She was initially a little slow, taking 15 minutes to do the easier ones, but as time went on, she moved onto the more advanced puzzles. She is certain her memory and timing have improved enormously because of it. She is excited by her progress, feels more energized, is more confident in trying new things, and is enjoying testing her brain again.

MIND OVER MATTER

Choose one or more of the following ideas to activate or quiet your mind. Remember 15 minutes is a starting point. Some of these suggestions might take longer especially if it's a project you want to achieve.

1. Meditate. Chant "Ohm" out loud and hold the Ohm till it runs out.

2. Turn your phone off for 15 minutes.

3. Take notice of the running to-do list in your mind and calm it by listing your thoughts on paper without restraint.

4. Read a book that has been sitting by your bedside.

5. Listen to an inspiring podcast or "Ted" talk at www.ted.com.

6. Actively engage someone in a stimulating conversation that you may or may not agree with—and really listen.

7. Watch a History, Discovery, or PBS station to learn something new.

8. Solve a brain-teaser. (Keep one with you to take out at any time).

9. Play Sudoku, Words with Friends, or Scrabble online.

10. Practice empathy. Put yourself in someone else's shoes to grasp his or her point of view when listening.

11. Write down all the pros and cons to a problem and discuss with a trusted friend.

12. Listen to the radio and call in to participate.

13. Read a magazine on a topic that you've been curious about and want to learn.

14. Take an IQ or EQ test online.

15. Engage in brainstorming with a friend or co-worker about a situation or conflict you are facing. Come up with as many solutions as possible in 15 minutes, and choose one to try.

16. Write an opinion piece you are passionate about and send it or email it to a blog or newspaper, maybe it's educational, social or political.

17. Learn a poem or funny joke and tell it at a party.

18. Start or end your day by consciously thinking about what brought you joy, write it down and keep a running tally.

19. Make a list of all the places you want to visit one day.

20. Play a card game to improve your memory.

21. Start a discussion on a current event
    that is going on in the world.

22. Cultivate silence, still the mind for 15 minutes you might
    be surprised by what ideas are waiting to come through.

23. Find a flower and focus on it to see all its beauty
    for a solid 15 minutes- next do it with a friend
    or loved one - focus on their beauty.

24. Listen to classical music, it is known for calming the mind.
    Absorb it and allow it to change your mood, play it back
    in your mind when you notice negativity creeping in.

25. Add one new word to your vocabulary
    each day and practice using it.

[1] Is silence golden? Effects of auditory stimuli and their absence on adult hippocampal neurogenesis, Imke Kirste, Duke University Medical School Dec 2013

[2] Ray Dalio: More than anything else I attribute my success to one thing, Julia La Roche May 2016

REFLECTION

How has putting one of these ideas into action made a difference to you?

Did taking 15 minutes help shift your mood? How?

How will you continue to calm or stimulate your mind daily, weekly, or monthly? Be specific.

"

Our body is
our temple and
knows what
it needs if we
listen to it.

"

CHAPTER SIXTEEN
BODY FOR LIFE

Feeding our body by maintaining good physical health and well-being is vital to surviving life's ups and downs. When we feel physically healthy, it's easier to move through the day with ease and grace. Staying fit and looking after ourselves are the cornerstones of dealing with the stressful demands of day-to-day living. Looking after our bodies means accepting our physical imperfections, after all, no one is perfect. When we can do this, it allows others to accept our imperfections as well.

Remember, you are special and unique. Just imagine what a monotone world it would be if everyone looked the same. Self-image and self-worth are inextricably linked, so learn to feed your body both from the inside and outside. What you feel on the inside will be seen on the outside. When you are unhappy or joyless, your posture, attitude, facial expressions, and body language reflect this to the outside world. Pay attention to how you really feel, after all, your body is your temple; look after it, and it will look after you.

It's vital to stay tuned into the Player, who urges you to practice looking after yourself. Don't wait until you are sick to take action. When you are unwell, it affects all other aspects of your life. Stay alert and be kind to yourself; after all, you are fabulous, beautiful and sexy irrespective of your body shape or size. When you look after your body, it's a sign of self-care and self-respect.

Meet Jen. She's a busy professional who spends many hours at work, leaving little time for herself and her physical fitness.

She felt stressed out and was not eating healthily or exercising. Jen shared her dilemma with Michelle, who mentioned what she had achieved in 15 minutes. Jen loved the idea and took the plunge to do something good for herself—starting with 15 minute walks. Soon she noticed a difference in her mental outlook as well as her physical self. Jen now walks regularly, has lost weight, and has started to nourish herself inside and out.

MOVE IT

Decide on one or more of the following ideas and start today to take better care of your body.

1. Go for a jog or walk - notice the flowers, trees, buildings.

2. Practice yoga at home. Start your day by stretching your body—really stretch from head to toe.

3. Give yourself a facial.

4. Enjoy a luxurious bubble bath; add oils, salts and light candles and rediscover the joys of pampering yourself.

5. Give yourself a pedicure or manicure.

6. Laugh regularly, watch a funny video or call an uplifting friend.

7. Take a mini-nap to put the zip back in your step.

8. Start a mini decluttering session.

9. Move your body in different ways e.g. Hula-hoop, or dance.

10. Make a change to your diet. Plan a week of healthy meals and snacks, find a cookbook for 15 minute dinners.

11. Enjoy a little "afternoon delight."

12. Sit in the sunshine and get some natural vitamin D.

13. Walk a dog (it doesn't have to be yours. Ask a neighbor or friend if you can walk his or her dog).

14. Stand in front of the mirror. Write down 10 physical aspects that you love about your body from your head to your toes and reread it to remind yourself.

15. Go outdoors: rake leaves, build a snowman, shovel snow, or mow the lawn to be more active and get outside.

16. Go to bed a little earlier than usual.

17. Go online and buy fancy lingerie that makes you feel good wearing it.

18. Incorporate mini meditations into your day.

19. Give yourself a mini-makeover or ask a friend to give you one.

20. Be silly, play or 'goof around' and let your inner child out.

21. Call a spa and book an appointment for a treatment.

22. Soak your feet in Epsom salts and release the tension.

23. Jump rope for 15 minutes - you will feel a difference if you do this regularly.

24. Put 2 tablespoons of safflower, argan or olive oil in your hair and let it sit for 15 minutes then wash out or sleep in it overnight. It will increase the shine.

25. Choose one area to work on. Do 50 sit-ups, or leg lifts and build your muscles 15 minutes each day.

REFLECTION

What key learnings do you have after reading this chapter?

How has your physical well-being helped your mental well-being?

If you continue to re-energize your body, what percentage increase do you think you will see a month or six months from now? Go back to the life energy inventory, and retake it in three or six months to find out.

> **"**The clearest message that we get from this 75-year study is this: **Good relationships keep us happier and healthier.** Period.**"**

— **Robert Waldinger,**
Director of the Harvard Study of Adult Development

Harvard's Grant and Glueck Study for over 75 years, tracked the physical and emotional health of two groups:

• 456 poor people in Boston between 1939 to 1945 (the Glueck Study)

• 268 sophomores from Harvard's classes of 1939–1944 (the Grant Study)

After following these groups and testing them (e.g., blood samples, brain scans) for several decades, the findings have been compiled. The study found that good relationships are the common factor for happiness and health.

"

Nuture love and it will grow.

"

CHAPTER SEVENTEEN
HEART CONNECTION

Healthy and harmonious relationships take time to grow and need
to be constantly nurtured, ignited, considered, and appreciated.
We all want to be loved, acknowledged and valued. This chapter
focuses on how well we practice coming from our heart when
we relate to our family, friends and others in our lives. How you
treat yourself sets the stage for every other relationship.

Every relationship is unique. The one you have with your
partner is different from the one you share with your children,
friends, parents, work colleagues, and yourself. Each relationship
needs heartfelt time and attention to flourish and grow.

When we take our relationships for granted, they suffer and this can
build resentment and anger over time. There are many reasons for
why this occurs. The lack of consideration and miscommunications
create conflicts when we spend more time working and caught in
the technology trap, on the phone or computer, rather than with
our family, friends and kids. When this happens too often, we can
feel ignored, cheated and dissatisfied. Other common reasons
include our unrealistic expectations of those we love. When we
put our hopes and beliefs in others and expect them to live up to
our ideals without expressing what we want out loud, we strain
our relationships and set ourselves up for further conflict. It is
very important to stop judging yourself and others. Let go of any
thoughts that say, "they must do this or they must be that."

Terri and her husband have been married for fifteen years and have two teens. After focusing on their kids' needs for the past ten years, they realized they had started to drift apart. They had taken each other for granted and forgotten to give their relationship the attention it needed because their energy was focused on the kids, their stressors and day-to-day life. They realized the kids were getting older and spending more time with their friends. Today, they have a weekly date night to reignite the passion and remember who they fell in love with. Each week they plan a special night together whether it's dinner out or cuddling at home watching a movie. This quality time is theirs alone to spend unplugged with each other.

NURTURE

Creating deeper more harmonious relationships is time well spent. If you want to increase your level of intimacy, acknowledge what your loved ones mean to you. Build in time with the emphasis on quality rather than quantity. Think about it: fifteen focused minutes with a child, a partner, or friend means far more than a distracted hour with phones ringing and texts being sent.

At the end of the day, how do you want to be remembered? Is it for working, rushing to the next appointment, being caught up in your to-do's, or is it for funny, joyful, surprising moments with the people in your life? Consider what matters most to you.

Here are some ideas for nurturing your most important relationships.

1. Switch off the phone and spend quality time focused on yourself, or your nearest and dearest.

2. Leave work 15 minutes early to meet a friend, partner or go home to your loved ones.

3. Surprise your lover or friend with flowers.

4. Call your grandparent(s) or a favorite aunt or uncle whom you haven't spoken to in a while.

5. Purchase "thinking of you" cards, or an online card and make someone's day by sending one out.

6. Call a friend. Reconnect with someone you've lost touch with.

7. Get your sexy back - e.g., take a shower with a partner or buy sexy lingerie.

8. Buy tickets for a show, a ball game, or a movie, and send one of them to a friend or loved one inviting him or her to join you.

9. Make ice cream sundaes at home with family or friends.

10. Acknowledge the great job your parent, child, or loved one is doing. Thank him or her sincerely.

11. Write a love letter and send it.

12. Spend time with a child and ask about his or her day. Really listen.

13. Play games e.g. Personalogy card game, outdoor game or Wii with your children or loved ones.

14. Turn off the TV, phone and computer and have a meaningful conversation with family or friends.

15. Cook with your children or loved ones; let everyone do something to contribute.

16. Be playful, have a joke-telling contest or pillow fight with your kids or loved ones. See which one of you laughs the hardest.

17. Start the day with a smile and hug, no complaints or negativity.

18. Be flirtatious with your partner, or if you are single, flirt with someone you like, or send a flirty text.

19. Create a romantic moment, turn on some music dance with your partner or put on fun dance music with your kids and have a dance off.

20. Take a leisurely stroll or bike ride with your partner, friend, or kids.

21. Connect with your community e.g. extend yourself to your neighbor by dropping off freshly baked cookies, scones or flowers from your garden, to say hello or thanks.

22. Join online dating site or meet-up to be social and meet new people.

23. Say "I love you" to all the people in your life that matter most to you.

24. Ask yourself "how can I be kinder to myself?" Write down everything that comes up.

25. Enjoy a "make-out" session or kiss and cuddle a partner.

REFLECTION

What can you do differently to spend more quality time with your loved ones?

What aha's have you learned to maintain harmonious relationships?

Have you made a heartfelt connection with someone in your life today?

"

Bless the past
and let it go.
Bless the future,
knowing it
has endless
joys. Bless the
present; I live
fully in the now.

"

CHAPTER EIGHTEEN
REWARD YOUR PROGRESS

Congratulations! Pause, now. Take a few moments and really acknowledge yourself for all the work you have done, the changes you have made and the new commitments you have pledged. Be proud of how far you have come.

Think of where you were when you started this playbook and where you are now. Reflect on what you have learned and achieved along the way. Did you break a negative pattern, add more fun or shift a mindset? Are you calmer or more energized?

How does it feel?

Also, thank your accountability partner, friend or loved one who has been with you on this journey. Celebrate, have a glass of champagne or sparkling apple cider, or do something special for yourself.

This is your time to validate how far you've come and the progress you've made so far. Personal acknowledgment along the way is vital to moving forward and staying on track.

Let's take a moment and recap to find out what aha's and reflections you've had over the course of reading this playbook. What takeaways come to mind, what are you aware of, what have you learned and gained on your path to better self-care?

MY FAVORITE AHA'S

Write down as many aha's as you can think of now. Try not to go back to what you wrote in the reflections, just go with your gut about what comes to mind. Use the whole page if you like. For example: I have a lot of negative mind chatter. My decisions have a consequence. I put myself on my to-do list. I'm more aware of my physical stressors. I let go of an emotional trigger. I think about the PPQ's before making a big decision.

After reading through Part One, Self-Awareness, Part Two, Conscious Choices and Part Three Purposeful Action, you are now equipped to create your personal i-Matter Equation below.

PAUSE

Think about one area you'd really like to change, one that matters most to you. Maybe it's related to your lowest score from the Life Energy Inventory™ or it's based on one of the previous chapters you've read.

Take a moment now and reflect on what one change would significantly impact your life in a positive way. This is your living reminder to say "yes" to yourself and "no" to the distractions, the sabotager and negative Meddler who want to make excuses.

i-MATTER EQUATION™

Self-Awareness + Conscious Choice + 15 Minute Pause = i-Matter Equation™

SELF-AWARENESS

*I am exhausted, work has become my priority,
I don't spend enough time with loved ones*

CONSCIOUS CHOICE

*I want to spend more time with people that
matter most to me regularly*

+

15 MINUTE PAUSE

*Leave work on time twice a week,
call a friend, plan a night out, switch off phone
and have face to face interaction*

=

i-MATTER™

More quality time for my relationships

SELF AWARENESS

+

CONSCIOUS CHOICE

+

15 MINUTE PAUSE

=

i-MATTER™

i-MATTER

I put myself
on my to-do list

PROGRESS ROAD MAP

Now that you have your personal i-Matter Equation™ completed, it's time to use the weekly progress worksheet on the following page to help you stay on track in the weeks and months ahead. It is designed to show you the progress you are making e.g., implementing better coping strategies, monitoring barriers and adding joy daily.

The worksheet is designed to capture the highlights of what you are doing weekly to make the changes you say you want fifteen minutes at a time. We suggest that you make a copy of this and plot your progress week by week over the next thirty days and into the future. Put it on your fridge, at your desk, or carry it with you to review and monitor. Also, be sure to give it to a friend or confidante to gain support, share ideas and successes. It helps when you have a partner along the way,

This is a useful tool to notice the changes you are making. It will give you a visual reminder of where you've been and how far you have come. This is an opportunity to be more observant of stressors, increase your self-care and notice more joyous moments in your life.

PROGRESS ROAD MAP

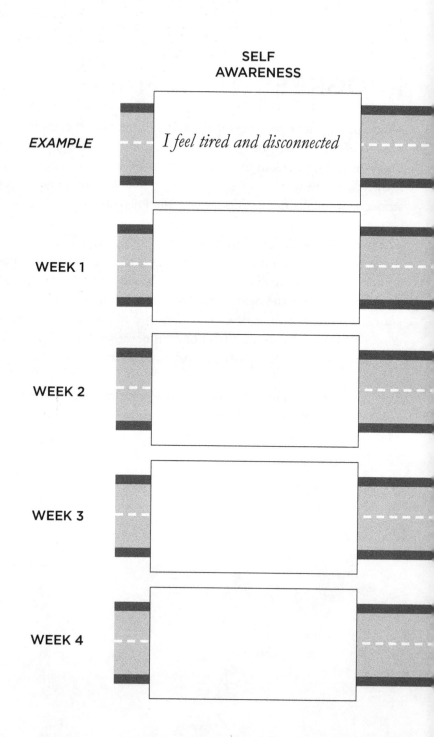

SELF
AWARENESS

EXAMPLE

I feel tired and disconnected

WEEK 1

WEEK 2

WEEK 3

WEEK 4

CONSCIOUS CHOICE	15 MINUTE PAUSE
Schedule time weekly for my relationships	*Leave work early, make plans with friends or family, switch off my phone and enjoy face to face interaction*

FINAL THOUGHTS

A LIFE WELL LIVED

Thank you for reading *15 Minute Pause* and congratulations for taking this valuable time for yourself. Our story is shared with you to show you that if we can do it, so can you. We would love to hear from you about what you discovered, your insights and aha's.

We learned that by being introspective we gained a greater understanding of how we feel, who we are, and what we want. The reality is that we still get stressed and exhausted and there are days when we forget to take a pause. It's not always easy, the difference is that we are more mindful today. We recognize the negative Meddler when it rears its ugly head and can stop it from taking over for days on end. We focus more on the Player voice and listen intently to make conscious decisions that are in our best interest.

Our positive choices show us that we can take better care of ourselves in a kind and compassionate way. Regular time-out helps us to reframe, giving us the chance to breathe, recognize joy and deal with everyday busyness in a more manageable way. We hope this book has done the same for you.

15 Minute Pause gives you permission to live your precious life in ways that matter most to you. It emphasized the value of 'me time'. The message to take dedicated time to reflect, de-stress and to keep your energy tank full is essential to your well-being. The purpose was to help you have a more fulfilling and less exhausted life. This is not about fixing yourself rather it's an opportunity to make small positive changes that benefit you over the long term.

We provided tools, antidotes, activities and resources to guide you to increase self-awareness, make conscious choices and take quality time for yourself. What have you gained, what have you let go of, and what are you doing differently?

The process of change isn't typically easy, and at times can be monumental. Yet, we have these grand ideas that we can snap our fingers and make things happen quickly, when often it can be slow and sometimes frustrating.

It will take patience and courage to reboot old familiar habits, leave your comfort zone, and pause long enough to put yourself first. Change happens when the benefits outweigh the cons. And, the key to long lasting change - the belief that you are worth the time and effort.

This is why the i-Matter Equation is so important. It is your personal promise to yourself to create the life you want, despite your other demands, errands, and stressors.

Your personal i-Matter Equation™ is a reminder to stay on your new path. It encourages you to put yourself on your 'to do' list. When your stress levels are in overdrive, don't be tempted to do more of the same - pause instead. Implementing 15 minute pauses daily remind you, that you are a priority.

We know from personal experience that taking care of ourselves can be challenging, however, the rewards are worthwhile. Most likely you've had to make some tough decisions, like leaving work on time or switching your phone off when with family or friends. When the busyness persists, remember the profound instruction on an airplane that was discussed at the beginning of the book. By now, you know that self-care begins with you. It's a simple fact that you can't help others if you don't refill your own cup first.

When your energies are drained and out of balance in one area, the consequences can be seen in other areas, lowering resilience and your ability to notice the 'good stuff' that is in your life. As we know now, poor excuses like 'I'm too stressed to manage my stress' are no longer welcome, since you have the Player to remind you to be accountable. To guarantee success start and end your day in gratitude or with an act of kindness.

Your daily pause is sacred. It's 'me time' to inspire you to slow down, reflect, relax, or add some sparkle to your life. What did you do with your 15 minutes today? Was the time calming, heart-warming or energizing?

We encourage you to live in the present, be mindful of what is important and to notice the joyous moments along the way. Fill your life with these moments they add up and will inevitably support you when that rainy day comes. Integrate 'play' into your routine more often, life is too short not to. When you are at a cross roads ask yourself the PPQ's, they will steer you in the right direction. And, remember to acknowledge your innate gifts, as these gifts are what make you unique and powerful.

This is an opportunity to create the life you declared you want. Dream Big. Prioritize the Player and stay aware of the Meddler's negative mental chatter. After all, *trying to do everything* on your to-do list or being available 24/7 doesn't work anymore. The wise Player realizes that you can't do everything and be everything to everybody. It's vital to be there for yourself.

The ongoing journey is now in your hands. The good news is, you have the power to change what no longer works, because you have the awareness and tools to do so. We understand that change takes commitment. Will you be kind to yourself along the way without guilt or sabotage? This is your time to give back to the most important person in your life—you.

Trust in the process and realize that you have the capacity to follow your heart, access your creativity, and stay true to yourself in a meaningful way. It's important to celebrate your successes, no matter how large or small. The less time you spend stressed and exhausted, the more time you have for what matters most, whether it's to enjoy the warm sun on your face, a moment of peace, or a hearty laugh with a loved one.

We continue to take our 15 minute pause daily, and we encourage you to do the same... notice the joyous moments, be grateful, so that when you look back, you can simply say, "I lived a joy-filled life, one worth living."

" Your time is now. "

TAKE THE PLEDGE.

Are you willing to take a pledge
and implement your i-Matter Equation™?
Complete the pledge below.
Take this pledge with someone else or alone,
committing to 15 minutes every day just for you.

15 MINUTE
pause

I commit to and deserve to take "me time"
pledging to take 15 minutes each day for myself
to enrich my life to the fullest.

_____   _____

Signature   *Date*

WE'D LOVE TO
HEAR FROM YOU

Tell us your stories about what you gained,
changed, learned, and achieved.

Connect with us at www.15minutepause.com or on FB https://
www.facebook.com/15MinutePause/ or Twitter @15minute-
pause or Instagram

"

Change is automatic. Progress is not. Progress is the result of conscious thought, decision, and action.

"

— Anthony Robbins

APPENDIX

Career/Financial Aspirations

75-100: Joy-filled. Well done!

Congratulations! Those who scored high are making a solid living doing what is meaningful or what they love doing. They purposefully take steps to make it happen. Furthermore, they realize that having work that has meaning is important. They continue to look for ways to improve or expand their learning and growth. It is a high priority to feel passionate about it.

They seek resources like a coach, financial advisor, people to connect with in the industry and continue to network in a variety of ways to keep improving and getting better. Those who are fulfilled in this area take classes or sign up for training to improve their skills or expand their experience. They are aware of their finances and take time to invest properly and save money along the way. They might also be a mentor to someone else to help them find more meaning in their career. They know how to use social media to stay connected and to keep up with the latest in the industry. They also read blogs, articles and other information to stay informed. Ultimately, they are energized and joy-filled as a result. They have the ability to help others if choose to and are aware of what is required to stay fulfilled in their career.

51-74: On the joy-filled track, requires attention

Those in this area know their career is important but want to be doing more of what they love and enjoy rather than doing work that doesn't have real meaning. They are generally satisfied with what they are doing. Yet, some may feel there is something missing. They may be unsure of what they want and the career path they are on right now.

If you are on the lower range of this scale, start with small easy 15 minute steps. Update your resume, brainstorm ideas with friends or associates. Reflect on what you want and write your thoughts down in a pro's and cons column. See what shows up. Seek out a career coach or mentor to help rethink options about how to incorporate current skills and experience. Research activities like networking events. It's vital to remember when attending a networking event to maintain a positive attitude because you never know when you might meet the right person that potentially leads to your next opportunity. Keep an open mind. Instead of thinking of it as a waste of time, consider what positive outcomes you got out of it.

Read books or blogs in the industry that you want to work in, or take a career assessment to find out what else you might be good at doing. When in transition, surround yourself with people who are positive and have your best interest in mind. If you want to change careers or launch a new endeavor, remember it requires time and patience. For those who are concerned about their finances, seek a financial advisor, call the credit card company and ask to lower your interest rate or start saving money. Put $1, $5 or $10 a day in a jar and take it to the bank each week, or set up an automatic transfer from your checking to your savings account. The main point to remember is you don't need to remain stuck. Take 15 minutes each day to reflect on what you want, and keep in close contact with your support network to stay motivated and on track.

0-50: Depleted, needs your attention

Those who are in this area may feel stuck in a career or lifestyle that has little rewards and/or little pay. They may want to do something else and might not have any idea of what that is or how to figure it out. When energy is low, the negative thoughts and excuses we have can dominate our thinking and, therefore, keep us stuck. Be aware of these red flags, like negative self-talk, lethargy and inaction. Take this opportunity to change the status quo.

The good news is change is possible and you have the power to make it happen. Give yourself the space to reflect regularly, put a time and date in your journal. Commit to 15 minutes and uncover what you want to do. Make a list of all the things you really enjoy doing, and don't hold back. One of these ideas may be a viable option and a positive way to create change or it may mean you need to dig a little deeper. Doing nothing only hinders us from moving forward.

Engage a coach, mentor, or financial advisor. Or, sit down with a friend and brainstorm ideas on what steps to take next. It might be interesting to think back to when you were a child and consider what you loved back then, list down your ideas in free form for 15 minutes. There are lots of free career assessments online. Check out Strengths Finder or Strengthscope.com to help you learn about your innate strengths. Read books to clarify your thoughts like "What Color is your Parachute"? There are many to choose from. If finances are the main issue or concern, then seek help from your banker. It's a free service, and they can set up an automatic transfer to help you save even if it's $10 per week or month. Call the credit card agencies and ask them to lower your interest rates, even if one says yes, that is a saving. Stop buying coffee or lunch and bring it to work instead and put that money in a jar and take it to the bank. If you feel you aren't earning enough, think about your value and worth.

What is most important is that you get the support you need. Start with one small action each day to help you progress. The more you do, the more energetic you will feel and the more likely you are to see positive results. You can do it!

Soul-Purpose

75-100: Joy-filled - Well done!

Congratulations! Those in this area consider this a high priority in their life. They have an innate awareness of what is needed to nurture their soul. They have spent time reflecting on what they want from life and know their life purpose. The activities they engage in fulfill their souls, whether it's time spent going to a religious or spiritual place to pray, meditate or spend time alone thinking. They know what it means to love and respect themselves.

People with these high scores understand how to actively participate in maintaining a healthy connection to the soul (there are many names for this – higher power, spirit, inner voice, God, Allah, Buddha, Muhammad, and have an inner strength that can be accessed anytime, no matter what chaos, fear or uncertainty is going on around them. They are proactive in their approach to life, and people enjoy being around them as they radiate positive energy.

Yet, they know the value of spending time alone. They understand that being alone is not the same as being lonely. When they take care of their inner needs, the ripple effect is felt in every other aspect of their lives from their relationships to their career, mind and body. This attitude helps them to cultivate a healthy and joy-filled lifestyle. Overall, they are deeply aware and able to make conscious choices that help them to stay joy-filled. Well done!

51-74: On the joy-filled track, requires attention
Those in this area connect on a soul level periodically and to varying degrees. They recognize the importance of taking care of themselves inside and out, yet are at times inconsistent. This inconsistency can result in a drop in energy levels. When this happens, it is then more difficult to bounce back from day to day problems. They may notice an increase in negative mind chatter, or they may argue and quarrel more often. These red flags indicate that other obligations, to do's, and stressors have taken precedence over what brings joy and calm. This is an indication that they need to start prioritizing time for themselves and the things that matter in their lives.

The good news is when we realize the value of being soul-filled, we will notice the joy it brings. However, those who are low in energy have to remind themselves to give this area the attention it needs. Make the time to nurture the soul on a daily or weekly basis. Put a date in your diary just for yourself. Start with a gratitude list, and write down what you like about your life. Try spending time alone in a peaceful and quiet place, be kind to yourself daily, and write down what you love about yourself and your life.

Appreciate you are unique. Put aside 15 minutes to pray, or meditate, talk to a minister or mentor and ask them for help to get reconnected. Or simply close your eyes and tune into your surroundings and be truly present. It is essential to take the time to feed your soul from the inside out. When you are strong at your core, the negative influences you encounter from outside have much less impact. Build inner resilience today.

0-50: Depleted, improve self-care
It simply means that the soul's energy levels are drained and those in this category need to spend focused attention here. It is not uncommon for those in this area to feel there is something missing, yet they might be unaware of what is missing.

They may be more likely to feel emotionally disconnected, may quarrel more often, and may feel lonely even when they are with people. Consider these red flags, and a sign that the soul requires nurturing. We may start to feel this way when other priorities, and a busy lifestyle prevent us from pausing and recovering. Increase inner strength and overall wellbeing, one small step at a time, 15 minutes a day.

Start being kinder to yourself and appreciate you are unique. Write a gratitude list daily add to it, or hang it on your mirror. There are books on finding your soul purpose as well. Those who want to discover their purpose can start by writing a list of what makes them happy. Try not to set any limits - just write. Keep in mind that those who make time for themselves have a greater capacity to give back to others. Take the time to put yourself first regularly. Be aware of the increase in negative self-talk and practice listening instead to the positive internal voice. This will increase your inner strength, self-respect and self-worth.

It is well documented that those who are happy on the inside at their core, are better at coping with negativity from the outside. Research shows that to function positively, every negative thought should be balanced with two positive thoughts. Continue to build on this. If unhappy with a relationship past or present, try forgiving them and accept the past is past. Concentrate on being in the present. Make a promise to stop looking backwards so you can continue to move forward in joy. Ask a friend or loved one to join you in discovering what makes them joy-filled. Your relationships, health and well-being are dependent on the choices you make today.

Philanthropy

75-100: Joy-filled. Well done!
Congratulations! You consider giving back a high priority and find ways to be philanthropic. Those in this area enjoy volunteering or find other ways to help those who are less fortunate than themselves. As a result, they are content with their philanthropic lifestyle. They are aware that by giving back, they also gain in return. They find unique opportunities to make someone else's life easier. For example, they may put extra money in a parking meter, help at their local community center, may give the homeless money or food.

They take the time to give to their favorite charities and may show up and lend a hand in their neighborhood. Whatever the action, they make conscious choices to be proactive. They are driven as they care about others and value this aspect of life. Many are boosted by the joy they receive in return and this in itself is fulfilling. Their energy levels are generally high. Keep up the good work!

51-74: On the joy-filled track, requires attention.
Those in this area give back in varying degrees. They care about doing well for others, however, they do it when it is convenient. Their priorities may lie elsewhere, and they extend themselves when the opportunity comes up. Some may feel it's difficult to give to others when they need to help themselves first.

The benefit is that by giving back, they can get back in unexpected ways that can be joy-filled. That said, most will give in whatever way makes sense at the time. Those who want to give and don't may suffer from guilt feelings because they haven't given enough. This is an indicator that giving back more often will be of benefit. The good news is there are easy ways to give back that don't require a lot of time or money. For example, paying someone's toll over a bridge or putting your change in the Red Cross box at the grocery store or buying food for a homeless person. Other ideas include bringing soup to a sick neighbor, or going by an assisted living place and bringing flowers. These are small ways of giving back that make a big difference in someone else's life; thereby, increasing your philanthropic well-being. Remember, how good it feels to help someone else, and it will make you feel good about yourself as well.

0-50: Depleted, needs your attention

It simply means that your philanthropic life is in need of attention. Those who find themselves in this category might be struggling to be philanthropic and may not be in the best place to help others. When they do give back, they may do so by writing a check because friends in support of a cause have brought it to their attention. Otherwise, being philanthropic is not a priority as they may feel there are too many other things to do, or they are not financially in a position to give. Many of us feel it has to be a big gesture, like giving a large amount of money or time. Think again. We believe there are many ways to be philanthropic and the good news is every little bit helps. If you want to increase this score and feel better about giving back, look for simple or easy ways to help in your neighborhood, community or church 15 minutes at a time.

Offer to drive someone to the Dr's office, donate clothes you don't wear to the charity shop, help a neighbor by bringing them food or medicine, give food to a homeless person or start to put a set amount of money aside (ten cents a day) for a cause and include your kids to make it a family experience. This helps to teach them about giving back at an early age, and the wonderful rewards of making a real difference in someone else's life. The beauty of giving back is that even a small change in attitude and action immediately increases energy and your family's energy. Enjoy!

Creative Catalyst

75-100: Joy-filled. Well done.

Congratulations! Those in this area are content and proactive when it comes to taking care of their creative needs. They recognize that by indulging in a creative endeavor, it adds more joy and fun. They are open to new possibilities and are always excited by what life can offer. Creative Catalysts take the opportunity to nurture this aspect of their life and actively participate in activities that feed their creative spirit. It is a priority to engage in tasks that recharge and boost their creative thinking and they make the time to unleash the creative child within, pursue a dream, craft or hobby. As a result, they are highly creative with abundant energy that is positive and, therefore, minimizing the negative mind chatter. Overall, people in this area make a conscious choice to stay creatively focused, follow their intuition and know how to reignite creative passions. They could help others by brainstorming ideas with them to tap into their creative energy. Well done!

51-74: On the joy-filled track, requires attention.
Those in this area consider it important to express their creative side but have good intentions to follow through however, they are more likely to do this periodically. If they are on the lower range of this scale, they may now be alerted to the fact that they haven't taken the time to be creative. This might result in increased stress levels, agitated feelings or increased negative mind chatter. These are indicators to foster the imagination to actively engage the creative catalyst within. Those who are at the higher range of the scale have a fairly steady level of creative energy as they take care of this aspect of life most of the time.

If you want to increase your creative energy, take 15 minutes to engage in a hobby, creative project, or learning something new. Whether it is listening to music, singing, blogging, painting or is a car enthusiast, indulge in a creative pursuit. If you have a larger project or a business idea, take small doable steps daily and build on this weekly.

You are now aware that 15 minutes equal to 91 or so hours a year – a lot of time to create and do what you want to do. In order to stay motivated, get the support of a friend or loved one who can encourage you to be more creative when depleted. Start increasing your creative energy today, find something you love, or have ignored and give it just 15 minutes of your time. Imagine the joy it will bring and you never know where it will lead. Good luck!

0-50: Depleted, improve self-care
Those who are in this area don't give their creative side expression or make it a high priority, although they wish they could. Their priorities are elsewhere, and they are unaware that their creative energy is depleted and needs refilling. Typically, they may not take action until it's too late. They may have excuses that may include a lack of time, other priorities, and a never-ending list of commitments and to do's to justify why they don't or can't take the time for a creative pursuit.

Simply put, they may consider it too difficult because they are stuck in fear, doubt or worry and this may stop them from being creative. Often, they don't start because of fear of failure or alternatively fear of success. Watch out for these red flags. Dig a little deeper to find out what is getting in the way. Try asking; "what stops you?" Write your answers down. Pay attention to the negative mind chatter. Is it dominating your thinking, and stopping you from proactively taking the initiative to give the creative "you" a chance to grow? Overall, if dreams seem unattainable, then think again. The restrictions we have are more often than not self-imposed.

Increase low energy levels in doable 15 minute increments. Imagine the fun you could have. Start by making a list of what you would like to do now- all ideas are okay. The main point is to let the creative juices flow. If you get stuck, ask a friend or family member to brainstorm with you. Choose a creative project that your family or a friend can join in and do it together. Maybe it's a home improvement idea, a plan to have a fun adventure with family or friends, the chance to use your camera again, write a poem, a song, or create a dream board. Find an area you want to reignite and take one step forward.

Remember that refilling your creative cup is important for living a more joy-filled life. When the creative mind is nurtured, the other areas like your relationships, health and well-being are improved. Be more aware of the choices you make. Start today by spending 15 minutes on a creative pursuit and see how it changes your life.

Power of the Mind

75-100: Joy-filled and self-aware - Well done!

Congratulations! Your mental well-being is thriving. People in this category are successful in utilizing their mind in ways that energize them and don't let the negative mind chatter get in the way. Those of you who have achieved a high level of mental energy typically understand the importance of learning and growing and actively participate in maintaining this aspect of your life. When you have high mental energy, you find opportunities to stay engaged in tasks that encourage and boost thinking whether it is reading, doing crossword puzzles or other mind-related activities.

Those with high mental energy tend to have the tools needed to quiet the mind through meditation, yoga or simply being in nature. When we have the ability to stay positive, we keep the negative mind chatter from taking over. When your mental energy becomes low, you do something about it. Overall, people with this high mental energy score are self-aware and make conscious choices to stay mentally alert and agile. They also know when they need to give their mind a rest, time to recover, to slow it down and pause. This time allows them to be more effective and alert when it is necessary. Continue to pay attention to keep your mental energy at a high level. Well done!

51-74: On the joy-filled track, requires attention

Those in this area manage their mental energy and well-being in varying degrees. As a result, they are inconsistent and less aware when they are exhausted or depleted. If this is where you are de-energized, make a note. Are you experiencing any of the following: hyperactive mind, negative mind chatter, boredom or do you wake up with a running to do list early in the morning? The majority of our problems begin when negative mind chatter starts to dominate our thinking.

The good news is we can increase awareness and do something about this when it happens. Learn to quiet the mind, and pause - meditate, pray, sit in nature, breathe or do yoga when the negativity appears. Overall, your mental energy levels are fair as you take care most of the time, yet it is the inconsistent approach that makes it difficult to maintain greater control. This is an indicator to put a regular routine in place to stay mentally alert and agile in your daily life.

When you find yourself with a drained brain, feeling confused, sleepless, unfocused or highly stressed, recognize these symptoms as mental fatigue. To re-energize, relax and slow the mind down, try listening to relaxing music, sit out in nature, or take a nap; to stimulate the mind read a book you have wanted to read for a while, listen to an interview or discussion on the radio or online, try puzzles, Sudoku, or challenge someone to a card or board game; these activities can be done in 15 minute increments if time is short and have the ability to rejuvenate mental energy levels quickly. It is important to find something that actively engages or disengages the brain if overall mental health is to be improved.

0-50: Depleted, improve self-care

It simply means that your mental energy is drained and in need of focused attention. Is it time to take action and make this a priority? It is not unusual to feel lethargic or have a short fuse because of the lack of time, work, and busy schedules that we call life. When mental energy is compromised, it impacts relationships and the ability to make conscious choices that are in our best interest. Be aware that mental energy is intimately associated with physical and emotional energy levels. When one area is low, it can influence the other areas of our lives. By improving this area, you will help boost the others.

The challenge is that when mental energy is this low, it's easy to justify why we don't or can't move forward to take care of our needs. Stay tuned into your negative mind chatter as it can start to dominate your thinking. The good news is you can take the initiative to change this attitude. Build in recovery time into your schedule. Start by making small doable changes 15 minutes at a time to quiet the mind. Try meditating, take a 15 minute nap or simply close your eyes, listen to a podcast, write your thoughts down without restraint, relax your mind by going for a walk in nature taking a bath or swim. If your mind needs more stimulation, read a book, call a friend, research a subject you have an interest in or a place you want to visit, or brainstorm a problem with a friend to get it off your mind.

For those who are stuck in negative mind chatter and think they have no way out we suggest you seek professional help from a doctor, a therapist, coach or minister. To keep you on track, ask family, friends or a co-worker to support you in your efforts to relax or to engage in improving your mental energy. Start making change happen today.

75-100: Joy-filled and self-aware - Well done!

Congratulations! Your physical energy is high. People with these high scores understand the value of taking good care of their bodies and physical well-being. They are aware of negative physical symptoms when they appear like a headache or sore throat and do something about it; like taking time out for a walk, removing themselves from the stress, having a break, taking time to eat lunch, adding fruit to their diets, or building in time for regular care like a monthly massage. They are more proactive and know the value of keeping their body active, eat regular meals, and take care of their sexual life, in ways that matter to them. They like their bodies and have a positive attitude to body and weight.

They feel physically healthy and are generally happy with their physical energy levels. They may suffer from aches and pains in their bodies and may have times when energy levels drop, yet they have an innate awareness to stop and recover before pushing forward again. They understand the need and value of resting and relaxing. It is this increased awareness that promotes better physical health overall, and allows them to take action to re- energize and regain balance when necessary. Well done.

51-74: On the joy-filled track, requires attention

Those in this area vary in how they manage their physical health. A lack of awareness may be responsible for this inconsistency. Often when our priorities lie elsewhere or we are distracted by our busy lives, we forget to put in place time for what matters most. Those who realize they need to improve their lifestyles may recognize the signs when they either feel exhausted, depleted or unwell.

If this area is where you are de-energized, make a mental note. Are you experiencing any of the following: Ongoing lethargy, is your stomach in knots, has your sex drive decreased or do you wake up tired? These are red flags and an indicator to put a regular routine in place to increase physical energy levels. The positive news is, those who find themselves in this category are capable of change. Take the time to eat well, sleep more, pamper yourself with massages or a pedicure.

The changes you make here can impact other areas of life like your mind and emotional energy. Exercise is recommended and known to be good for us. Build it into your routine regularly. Start with 15 minutes a day, as it's easy and doable. Break a pattern and leave work early to take a walk, walk during your lunchtime. Or add 15 minutes of stretching before you go to bed. If you want to have more physical contact, give your partner, your friends or kids a big hug. Similarly, to improve your diet, buy yourself fruit and vegetables weekly and eat them daily. If you are trying to lose weight, take an apple to work or eat fruit as a healthy snack in between meals instead of chips or candy. Make a healthy evening meal 3-4 times a week. This will increase your overall well-being and up your physical energy levels.

As you begin to take better care, these small changes will get easier over time. Ask a friend or loved one to join you in your quest to increasing your physical fitness and health. Start taking care of yourself in small steps. The benefits will more than compensate for the effort you put in.

0-50: Depleted, improve self-care

When we find ourselves in this category, it simply means our physical energy is drained and in need of focused attention. It may be time to take action and make this a priority. It is not uncommon for those in this area to feel tired, lethargic, to be dissatisfied with weight or have issues with body image. When physical energy levels are compromised, it can impact our ability to make choices that are in our best interest. Be aware of excuses.

By improving this area, it will help boost other areas, like the mind. Look out for the red flags, like increased muscle tension and knots in the stomach, that alert us to stop and reassess the way we are living our life. Those who build in recovery time into their schedule have a greater chance of improving their well-being. The more positive ways we find to increase physical energy, the less likely we are to get sick or exhausted.

Increase energy levels by walking to work or do a fast 15 minutes around the block. Do this regularly 2-3 times weekly and add it into your journal to remind yourself. Instead of staying at your desk at lunchtime take in some sunshine, snack on fruit like avocados and nuts, which are excellent energy boosters. Nuts are a great alternative to sweet snacks, like candy, if you want to lose weight. Take care of your sexual health, ask friends to introduce you, flirt, or sign up for a dating site. Make an appointment for a mini-makeover or a haircut. Ask a friend to join you, and use this as an opportunity to create a goal to lose weight or get in shape, start taking care of yourself in small steps. Add one of these new routines to your week and notice the benefits.

Heart Connection

75-100: Joy-filled. Well done!

Congratulations your heart is full. Those in this area are content with their intimate relationships. As a result, they are in the main emotionally fulfilled. Yet we all know emotions and energy levels go up and down. The difference is those in this area actively participate in maintaining a healthy connection regularly. They know healthy relationships are cultivated and improved with constant effort and input. As a result, they make this aspect of life a priority. They know that time with family and their friends is essential to their wellbeing.

When their energy levels drop, they take action to do something about it e.g. like calling friends, spending time with those they love or leaving work earlier to be with their families. They recognize the importance of switching off from technology whenever possible to spend quality time with those that matter. If love or partnership is what they seek, they are actively looking for and making time for this. Overall, they make conscious choices to stay emotionally engaged and take good care of their relationships to satisfy their emotional needs and wants. Well done!

51-74: On the joy-filled track, requires attention

Those in this area have a fairly good understanding of what it means to maintain their relationships with those closest to themselves. This is reflected in their good intentions and promises, however, they are inconsistent. Overall, they know the value of spending time with loved ones, yet the inconsistency can at times create stress and dysfunction. Some of the red flags to look out for include: more arguments, or feelings of being disconnected. When we are able to nurture our relationships regularly, these feelings are less likely to occur. Learn to recognize the signs. Put a regular routine in place to stay emotionally connected. Try leaving work early to be with family or friends, have breakfast, lunch, or dinner around the kitchen table, switch off the TV and other electronic gadgets, and bring flowers to those you love. Take 15 minutes out to research ideas for a fun day out, like music concerts, weekends away with friends or family, or organize a date night. Get online and look for love, if that is missing in your life. Flirt when out, change a routine and go somewhere you don't normally go. This is your opportunity to make the most of your time to reignite your relationship with your loved ones.

0-50: Depleted, improve self-care

It simply means that the relationships we have with those in our life are in need of care and focused attention. Those in this area may have let their relationships go allowing them to drop down their list of priorities. As a result, they might have noticed that they are more emotionally disconnected from loved ones, have more conflicts and arguments, and may be lonelier. These "red flags" are an indication that something has to change. It is important that we recognize how our actions as well as our in actions, impact the relationships we have. Doing nothing is not the answer; in fact, it can be the reason why there is greater conflict or things are where they are.

Take time to pause, recover and nurture your relationships. Recognize that emotional energy is low at present. Those in this area can make genuine strides to improve their relationships by making better conscious choices. The good news is you don't need to spend hours to do this. Start by putting 15 minutes aside and call a friend, write a love letter, go online and buy something sexy to make yourself feel attractive. Send an email to your closest friends and invite them to a girl's night in, pick a movie and schedule a movie night, make popcorn with the kids, show genuine affection and give the ones you love a big hug. Try switching off your electronic gadgets, or leave work 15 minutes early and give those you care about quality time. For those who are single and looking for love, get online. Flirt when out, change a routine and go somewhere you don't normally go. If you need further help contact a doctor, therapist, counselor or minister. Your relationships, health and well-being are dependent on the choices you make. Start taking better care of your emotional energy and your relationships today.

GLOSSARY OF TERMS

Energy—a Greek word meaning activity.

i-Matter Equation — Self-Awareness + Conscious Choice + 15 Minute Pause. Having self-awareness (Introspection), making conscious choices (Decisions) and pausing for 15 minutes a day (Purposeful Action)

Joy-filled — Has self-worth. Values self-care and shows kindness to themselves. Has gratitude and is aware of joyous moments that show up, not stuck in worry, fear or doubt, manages stress, engages life fully and appreciates the present moment.

Self-Awareness — to be aware of and understand your needs, appreciate the simple pleasures, be mindful of your thoughts and beliefs and introspectively assess them to foster a positive mindset.

Conscious Choice — means being fully aware of your reality and the consequences and impact of your decision(s) before you make it, staying true to your values regardless of the internal or external pressures; recognizing your non-negotiable needs.

Pausing for 15 Minutes — Recovery time - focuses on stopping, reassessing and reframing life. It requires you commit to taking purposeful action: fifteen minutes at a time.

Joyous Moments — A funny, calming, and meaningful moment that is noticed, savored, and appreciated in everyday situations.

Priority Players Questions (PPQ) — a series of eight questions applied when creating a new routine, task or commitment. Used to help in the decision-making process to clarify whether something is a real priority or not.

Mental Energy — refers to the ability to be aware of your thoughts, to stimulate the mind in positive ways, gain knowledge, improve a skill, and promote a healthy mind-set.

Physical energy — refers to the awareness of how your whole body feels; it is the momentum for taking good care of your body, your response to handling pain and the action you take to have overall physical wellness.

Emotional energy — refers to the ability to perceive, assess and manage your feelings and emotions, as well as recognize other people's feelings and to respond in a healthy way.

Meddler — The negative internal voice in your head. The Meddler is a complainer who creates excuses, fears and barriers to keep you from doing what is right and best for you.

Player — The positive internal voice in your head. The Player voice is your cheerleader, friend, coach, and avid supporter.

Intelligence quotient (IQ) — is how quickly you absorb new information and is associated with the power of reason.

Emotional intelligence quotient (EQ) — a term coined by author Daniel Goleman, is a yardstick for measuring social and emotional awareness.

Innate Qualities — the unique gifts, talents and qualities we are born with that come to us naturally without effort or learning.

Mindful — ability to be aware of subtleties of human behavior including; facial expressions, body language and tone of voice.

Self-Care — when you take time to take care of your needs. And you keep your energy tank full before caring for others (example having a full tank of gas).

AUTHOR'S REFLECTION

LILAMANI'S STORY:

We all have defining moments. I grew up in Sri Lanka in a small rural town, and from the beginning, my parents always reminded me of how lucky I was. Poverty is ever present in Asia, and as a result I learned not to take what I had for granted.

Looking back, I can pinpoint a profound life experience that stands out for me at age five. There were no English-speaking schools in the small community we lived in so my parents made the tough decision to send me to boarding school, knowing this opportunity would serve me well in the future. The thought of going away from home, even if it was only five hours away, was daunting. Yet, I don't recall feeling abandoned as my parents were always loving, kind and generous.

On reflection, sending a five-year-old away from home was probably much harder for my parents than it was for me. Leaving home and the security that came with that was hard. I arrived to an environment very different to the one at home, where discipline was strict, timetables had to be followed, and children of all ages roamed the corridors competing for attention. I cried a lot, was scared and lonely. I missed my parents and siblings yet, as time went on I adapted, made new friends and settled into a routine. The school was run by nuns, the hardy, strict variety. One nun stands out. She loved to sing, and there was one song she sang ad infinitum "Que sera – what will be will be". It wasn't till much later in life that I realized that song and the philosophy of letting life flow had a significant impact on my thinking. In those three years I grew up quickly, learned to fit in, and realize now in hindsight, that I'd made a conscious choice to adapt. I realized, too, that I was resilient. These qualities helped me later at age eight, when I moved to New Zealand and had to assimilate to a very different lifestyle. These life lessons continue to serve me well on my journey.

MICHELLE'S STORY:

I grew up in Northern California in a small town with two younger siblings, a brother and sister. My parents raised us Catholic and we went to church on Sundays. I grew up believing in God and had a strong faith. Looking back, I was a creative and happy child with an active imagination, always dreaming up games with my siblings or writing plays for the neighborhood kids for us to perform. We moved every few years because my Dad worked in finance and was often promoted. By the age of ten, I had attended three different Catholic grammar schools. I struggled with being the new kid on the block and especially so going into 5th grade when my parents divorced. Upon reflection, that was one of the most difficult and defining times in my childhood. I cried often and was extremely upset about my parents and nervous about going to another new school. Arriving two weeks late, I remember feeling afraid that no one would like me or want to be my friend. Being shy and a bit awkward led me to the "misfit" group. It took months before I felt like I belonged. After weeks of eating lunch often by myself, I finally made friends with a girl with my same name. We became fast friends, and it was then that my life at school and thereby home started turning around for the better. Having a best friend made such a positive difference in my life.

What I learned is that life changes whether you are ready for it or not, and need to keep finding the good amid the "bad." I discovered that I wasn't alone. I enjoyed spending time with my friends and immersed myself in school work and reading. I found reading brought me great joy and it still does to this day. My faith carried me through the confusion, pain and sadness that I felt along the way. This was my saving grace. Throughout the many ups and downs, my gratitude for the small things, my faith in something greater than myself, and doing the things that I love continue to carry me through life. Most importantly, I now know what it is to look for the blessings and acknowledge what I am grateful for daily. These life lessons keep me firmly rooted in the present while enjoying the journey.

AUTHOR BIOS

Michelle Burke is a highly respected and sought-after leadership and team coach, consultant, strategist, and speaker. As Founder and President of Energy Catalyst Group, she has devoted her 20-year career to helping organizations become thriving energized workplaces. Her consulting and coaching with Fortune 100, 500 companies and Universities established her as a leading expert in bridging communication, team and cultural gaps. Her clients include: Sony PlayStation, Stanford University, Visa, Microsoft, Cisco Systems, Disney, HTC, Snap Inc., Genentech, and HP.

She is author of the acclaimed book, *The Valuable Office Professional,* endorsed by Ken Blanchard. She co-developed The Productivity Cycle™, a communication tool proven to enhance teamwork and increase productivity, endorsed by Stanford University.

Michelle is a member of Forbes Coaching Council and a participant in UCLA's Mindful Awareness Research Center (MARC) intensive IPP program. She has been featured in Business Week Magazine, Los Angeles Times, San Francisco Chronicle, Wall Street Journal, and Star Ledger. She was a regular contributor for Great Work Cultures on Huffington Post, and contributes to Forbes.com. Her articles have appeared in HR, Training and CLO Magazines. Michelle enjoys giving back to her community, traveling, reading, cooking and is a sports enthusiast.